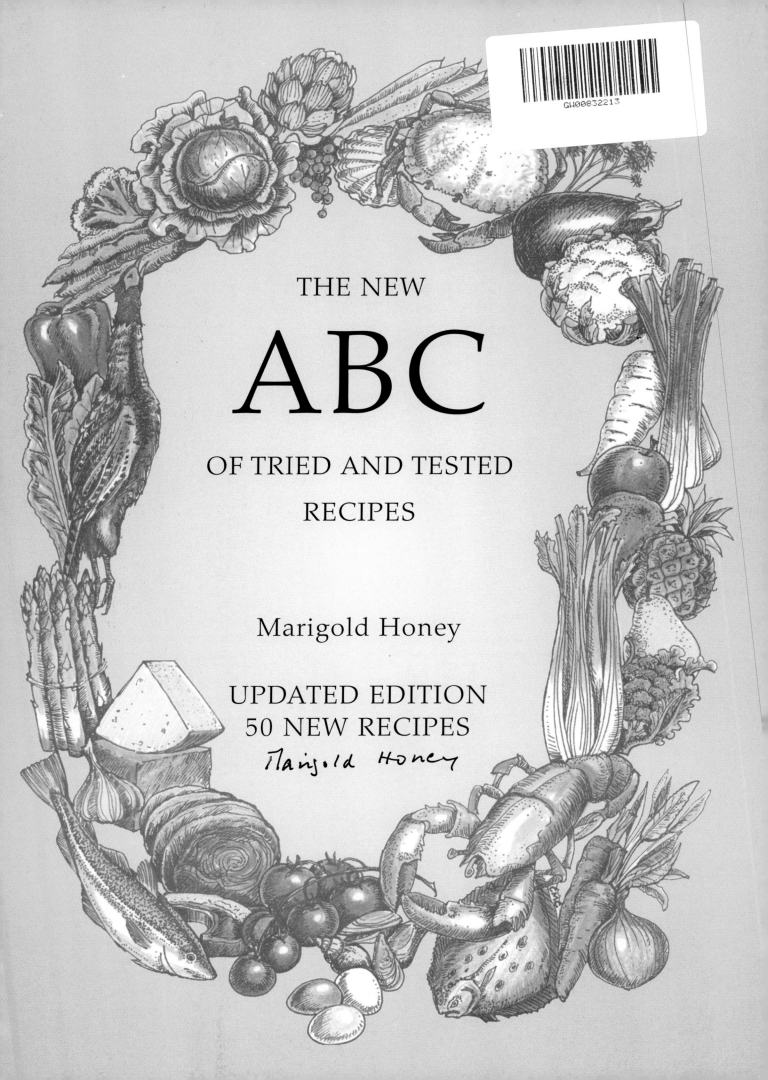

THE NEW

ABC

OF TRIED AND TESTED

RECIPES

Marigold Honey

**UPDATED EDITION
50 NEW RECIPES**

Marigold Honey

Published by Marigold Honey, Day`s Cottage, North Stoke, Oxon OX10 6BL

ISBN 978-0-9536306-1-5

Design by Stanley Codling
Illustrations by Carolyn Codling

Printed by Woodrow Press, Unit 1A, 28 Quebec Way, London SE16 7LF.

DEDICATED TO

MY MOTHER

AND

GRANDMOTHER

ACKNOWLEDGEMENTS

I would like to thank Stan Codling for designing the cover of this book, together with his wife Carolyn for the colour illustrations. I would also like to thank Rob Allen of Woodrow Press for his help with the printing of this book.   I am also very grateful to my family. My husband, Roger, who has eaten his way through all the recipes; my son, Luke, for his encouragement and advice; my daughter, Camilla, for her professional ideas regarding promotion and the Sargeaunts for the printing.

.

PREFACE TO NEW UPDATED EDITION

It is over ten years since I published my ABC Cookery book and as it has now sold out, I have decided to print a New Updated Edition. There are 50 new recipes and some of the old ones, with difficult to obtain ingredients, have been altered or removed. This is a recipe book rather than a cookery book for people who know how to cook and have to produce food day in and day out during the year. So many recipes in cookery books do not work, are not worth the trouble and are unnecessarily expensive. A great deal of time is wasted searching through different cookery books looking for recipes. Many of these recipes have been handed down, some are classics, others are my own invention and some have been given to me by friends.

People have found the recipes easy and quick to use and it is also of course an advantage that the majority of them can be made in advance. This is something I learnt from my mother. She always prepared her meals ahead as my father hated her being in the kitchen.

I hope this book will encourage people to eat at home without too much time, trouble and expense. Once again I would like to thank my family and friends for their help and encouragement.

Marigold Honey

June 2010

CATEGORIES

CHRISTMAS

COCKTAILS

FISH

FRUIT (See also under **PUDDINGS**)

LIGHT MEALS

MEAT

PASTA AND RICE DISHES

PETITS FOURS

PUDDINGS (see also under FRUIT)

XIII

SALADS

SAUCES

SOUPS

STARTERS

STORE CUPBOARD

VEGETABLES

ALMOND BISCUITS

3 oz (75g) soft butter
1½ oz (35g) brown sugar
4½ oz (120g) plain flour
1½ oz (35g) ground almonds
Tsp almond extract

2 ½ " (6 cm) cutter

Heart cutter and crystallised violet petals (optional)*

This idea came from my granddaughter!

Blend butter and sugar and stir in the flour and almonds and extract to form a dough or put all the ingredients in the magimix and turn on briefly. Cover the mixture in cling film and leave in the fridge.

Roll out the dough and cut into rounds and hearts. Prick well and decorate in the centre with violet petals if you have them. Bake at 200C/400F/Gas 6 until pale brown – about 8 mins. Leave to cool and then keep in an airtight tin.

ANCHOVY AND EGG MOUSSE (6)

6 Eggs
9 Anchovy fillets
Dsp powdered gelatine
2 tbsp sherry or water
Heaped tsp curry powder
Pinch cayenne
Ground pepper
10 fl oz (300 ml) double cream

Hard boil the eggs for 10 minutes, pour over cold water, peel and leave them in a bowl of cold water after peeling. This stops them going black round the yolks. Put the sherry in a ramekin dish, shake over the gelatine and stand in a saucepan in a little water over heat until it melts. Meanwhile sieve the egg yolks, chop the egg whites and mix with the anchovies (cut into tiny pieces), the curry powder, cayenne and black pepper. Beat the cream slightly, fold in the anchovy mixture and finally fold in the gelatine. Put immediately into individual ramekin dishes and place in the fridge. Serve with hot bread or rolls. Do not freeze as egg yolks turn to rubber in the freezer!

APPLES

See also:
       Chocolate Apples
       Chutney – Irish
       French Apple Flan
       Pancakes

APPLE AMBER

2 lb (1 kg) apples
3 tbsp granulated sugar
Rind and juice of half a lemon
Slice of butter
2 eggs, separated
4 oz (110g) caster sugar (for meringue topping)

Decoration: Glacé cherries, flaked almonds

Puree apples by peeling, slicing and cooking with the granulated sugar and lemon juice and a tablespoon of water.   Beat in butter a little piece at a time.   Cool and then stir in the egg yolks. Pour into a shallow ovenproof dish.

Make meringue by beating the egg whites until stiff, stir in a tablespoon of caster sugar, beat more until really stiff and then fold in the rest of the sugar.   Spread all over the apples, dust with caster sugar and for a special occasion, decorate with glacé cherries (halved) and flaked almonds.   Bake for about 20 minutes in a moderate oven until the meringue is brown.   Serve cold with cream.

APPLE CAKE

1 lb (450g) cooking apples
4 oz (110g) butter
4 oz (110g) caster sugar
4 oz (110g) plain flour
1 egg
2 tbsp sultanas
2 tbsp brown sugar
2 tbsp chopped nuts
1 tsp cinnamon
1 dsp lemon juice
Flaked almonds

Line a loaf tin with foil. Scatter the base with flaked almonds. Core, peel and slice the apples. Melt the butter and mix with the sugar.   Add flour and egg to make a batter. Spread half of the mixture on base of tin; cover with half of the sliced apple; cover with mixture of cinnamon, lemon juice, brown sugar and sultanas; cover with remainder of apples.   Finally, sprinkle with chopped nuts and spread the rest of the mixture on top.

Bake in a moderate oven for up to an hour till firm and brown.   Leave in tin for a little while and then turn out carefully onto a long plate. Serve cold in slices with cream.

APPLE CHUTNEY*

2 lb (900 kg) cooking apples or windfalls
2 tbsp salt
1 whole head of garlic, peeled
1 inch piece of ginger, peeled
4 fl oz (125 ml) cooking oil
2 tbsp mustard seed, 2 tsp cumin powder, 1 tsp fenugreek seed
1 tsp chilli powder, 1 tsp turmeric, 15 peppercorns
3 – 4 fresh green chillies, seeded and chopped
5 fl oz (150 ml) vinegar
4 oz (110g) granulated sugar

This is fairly spicy

Peel, core and slice the apples, sprinkling them with the salt and setting aside. Finely grate half the garlic and ginger and thinly slice the other halves. Heat the oil in a large pan. Fry the ginger and garlic. When starting to brown, add mustard and fenugreek seeds, peppercorns, cumin, chilli powder, turmeric and chopped chillies (removing seeds with a knife). Fry gently for a few minutes, then add the apples, vinegar and sugar. Stir well and cook slowly for about 30 minutes. Cool and put into screw-top jars.

Keep for a few months before eating. Good with cheese.

APPLE CRUMBLE*

2 lb (1 kg) apples
8 oz (225g) sugar
4 oz (110g) flour
4 oz (110g) butter
Tsp cinnamon

* This is a favourite dish, often hard to find in recipe books. It can of course be made with any fruit.*

Put fruit, peeled and sliced, into a deep ovenproof dish. Mix flour and sugar and add pieces of butter until like fine crumbs. Add a little water and a teaspoon of cinnamon to the fruit. Top with the crumble mixture, pressing down well with a fork, especially at the sides.

Bake in a moderate to hot oven for up to an hour till brown. Serve hot with pouring cream.

APPLE PIE

Pastry:
    8 oz (225g) plain flour
    2 tbsp caster sugar, pinch salt
    4 oz (110g) butter
    1 egg yolk mixed with 3 tbsp water

Filling:
    2 lb (1 kg) cooking apples
    5 oz (150g) granulated sugar
    Small tsp cinnamon
    1 tbsp marmalade
    Knob of butter

Make pastry either by hand or in a mixer, adding pieces of butter to flour, sugar and salt until like crumbs.   Add egg yolk mixture until like a paste. Chill. Peel and slice apples and cook with sugar and cinnamon to a puree.   Add marmalade and butter, beat well and cook for another 5 minutes. Divide pastry into two.   Line Pyrex pie plate or shallow flan dish with pastry.   Fill with apple mixture.   Cover with other half of pastry. Press edges down well, brush with the egg white and dust with sugar. Make a slit in the centre of the pastry to let the air out.   Decorate.

Bake in a hot oven 30 – 40 minutes. Serve hot or cold with cream. Can be frozen.

APPLE RAMEKINS (4)

1 lb (450g) apples
3 oz (75g) granulated sugar
2 tbsp water
Topping:
    2 oz (50g) butter
    2 oz (50g) sugar
    2 oz (50g) ground almonds
    Egg yolk

Peel and slice the apples and cook to a puree with sugar and water.   Put in small individual heatproof dishes.   Make topping by creaming the butter with the sugar.   Add egg yolk and ground almonds to make a paste. Either chill, roll out and cut into rounds or divide into balls and flatten. Place on top of the apples.   Cook in a moderate oven for 20 – 30 minutes.   Serve with pouring cream.   Leave to cool for a moment or two after taking these dishes out of the oven, as they will be very hot.

For an instant pudding, take apple puree from freezer or a tin of apple and blackberry, place in dishes and top with Demerara sugar, ground almonds and flakes of butter. Cook as above.

APPLE SAUCE*

1 lb (450g) apples
2 tbsp water, half a lemon
Tbsp sugar
Knob of butter

Serve with pork

Peel, core and slice the apples. Put in a saucepan with the water and lemon. Cover with buttered paper – taken from a slab of butter – put on the lid and cook till mushy.   Remove the half lemon, add sugar to taste (depending on the apples` tartness) and beat to a puree adding a knob of butter.

APPLE SNOW (4)

1½ lb (675g) cooking apples or windfalls
2 oz (50g) granulated sugar
2 tbsp water
2 egg whites
4 oz (110g) caster sugar
Cinnamon, lemon juice

Peel, core and slice the apples and put in a saucepan with 2 tablespoons of water. Cover with a buttered paper and a lid and cook slowly until soft and fluffy. Add the granulated sugar and mash to make a puree. Leave to cool.

Whisk the egg whites until firm and then add a tablespoon of the caster sugar at a time, continuing to beat until stiff and shiny. Fold in the apple puree, together with a pinch of cinnamon. Taste and add either some more sugar, if sour, or some lemon juice if too sweet. Put into four attractive glasses and leave in the fridge. Serve cold with biscuits.

APPLE STRUDEL

Packet of short filo pastry
Crisp tasty apples – e.g. Braeburn or Cox`s
Butter, brown sugar, sultanas
Chopped nuts, breadcrumbs, cinnamon
Rind and juice of ½ lemon

Take a leaf of the filo pastry, keeping the rest covered.   Brush with melted butter, fold over and brush again.   Peel and chop the apples and mix in a bowl with the other ingredients. Put a large spoonful of this mixture on the pastry. Turn in the sides and roll up. Continue with the rest of the pastry.   Place the individual strudels on a well greased Swiss-roll tin. Brush with melted butter.   Cook in a hot oven 400F/200C/Gas 6 until brown.   These can be kept in the fridge or frozen and then reheated.

APRICOT CHUTNEY*

1 lb (450g) dried apricots soaked overnight in 1 pint water
6 cloves of garlic, crushed
1 pt (570 ml) malt vinegar
1 lb (450g) brown sugar
5 level tsp ginger

This chutney is a little like a mango chutney – delicious with curries

Cook the soaked apricots with their liquid in a large pan slowly for about 20 minutes. Mix garlic, ground ginger and vinegar and add to the apricots with the sugar. Stir until the sugar is melted and then simmer for about 1½ hours till thick. Cool a little and put into screw-top jars.

APRICOT MOUSSE*

8 oz (225g) dried apricots, soaked overnight
Pared rind and juice of half a lemon
2 medium cooking apples, peeled and sliced
Sugar to taste
2 egg whites

A simple recipe without using cream or gelatine

Strain apricots keeping a little of the juice and stew gently with the apples, lemon juice and rind. Drain from the juice and rub through a sieve or liquidise. When cold, sweeten puree to taste. Whip egg whites and add by degrees to the puree, continuing to whisk.

Put in an attractive glass dish and scatter nuts or grated chocolate on the top.

APRICOT STUFFING

6 oz (175g) dried apricots, soaked overnight
6 oz (175g) fresh breadcrumbs
4 oz (110g) celery, finely chopped
1 large spring onion, or shallot, finely chopped
Tbsp butter, melted
Small egg
Salt, pepper, tbsp Dijon mustard

Drain the apricots and chop. Combine the apricots, breadcrumbs, celery, onion, and seasoning with the melted butter. Mix egg and mustard together and bind the stuffing.

Use to stuff joints or the Christmas turkey. It can be made the day before and kept in the fridge before stuffing the meat. Can be frozen, but better if freshly made.

APRICOTS WITH COCONUT

Fresh apricots (two per person)
Grated coconut or desiccated coconut
Coconut cream liqueur
Topping:
    Brown sugar
    Knob of butter

Halve the apricots and remove the stones.   Place in a shallow ovenproof dish, fill with the coconut and top with brown sugar and shavings of butter.

20 minutes before eating place them in a hot oven.   Remove when needed, pour over some coconut cream liqueur and serve.

ARTICHOKE BOTTOMS (4)

1 tin artichoke bottoms
8 oz (225g) mushrooms, peeled and sliced
2 red peppers, grilled and skinned
Herb dressing made with:
    1 tbsp wine vinegar,
    1 tbsp olive oil, 1 tbsp walnut oil
    1 tsp salt and sugar
    Chopped fresh herbs (e.g. parsley, chives etc)

Cut up bottoms and divide between four individual bowls. Add sliced mushrooms, well wiped and peppers cut into small dice.   Mix dressing and pour over. Add dressing about one hour before serving, if possible.

ARTICHOKE HEARTS (6 - 8)

2 tins artichoke hearts
3 eggs – hard boiled
French dressing made with:
    2 tbsp lemon juice
    3 tbsp olive oil
    Salt, pepper and sugar
Salad leaves

On individual plates or bowls, place hearts on strips of decorative salad leaves. Top with chopped egg white and sieved egg yolk.

Just before serving pour a little of the previously mixed dressing over carefully.   Serve with home-made rolls, warmed in a low oven.

ASPARAGUS

To cook fresh, first scrape the ends of the asparagus having cut off the bottoms. If using an asparagus pan tie in bundles and stand upright and steam for about 10 minutes. Otherwise place the bundles in a large saucepan lying down and pour over boiling water, with a little salt, to cover. Boil for 10 – 15 mins. until tender. Serve the asparagus with hollandaise sauce or with melted butter as a first course. Or serve with slices of smoked salmon and avocado for a main course.

ASPARAGUS FLAN

Shortcrust pastry:
    8 oz (225g) flour
    2 oz (50g) butter, 2 oz (50g) lard
    5 tbsp water
8 or more pieces of fresh asparagus or a tin of asparagus
1 oz (25g) butter
1 oz (25g) flour
5 fl oz (150 ml) milk and 5 fl oz (150 ml) asparagus juice
2 oz (50g) grated cheese (Cheddar or Parmesan)

Make shortcrust pastry, either in mixer or by hand, mixing small pieces of the fats into the flour and then making into a paste with about 5 tablespoons of water. Chill. Line a 9 inch (22 cm) flan dish and bake blind by lining the pastry with foil and baking beans and cooking for 25 minutes in a hot oven. Either cook some asparagus for about 10 minutes, reserving 5 fl oz of the cooking water or open a tin of asparagus. Melt the butter, add the flour, cook over the heat for a minute or two and then add the liquid, stirring until boiling. Pour sauce into the pastry case, place asparagus in shape of a wheel and cover with grated cheese. Reheat when ready to eat.

ASPARAGUS MOUSSE (6)

2 tins green tipped asparagus
7 fl oz (200 ml) double cream
1 pkt or 3 tsp gelatine
2 tbsp sherry or water
4 leaves gelatine
½ pint (300 ml) liquid from tins with little wine

Put asparagus in mixer with lots of seasoning and small amount of liquid from the tin. Mix 2 tbsp sherry and/or water with gelatine in small ramekin dish. Leave for a short while, then melt by standing dish in small saucepan over hot water. Whip the cream, add the asparagus puree and pour over the gelatine. Mix gently and put into 6 ramekin dishes. Leave to set in the fridge.

Soak the gelatine leaves in half a pint of liquid made up of juice from the asparagus tins and a little wine. Warm until the gelatine is dissolved, cool a little and then pour over the mousses. If desired decorate with some asparagus tips. Leave to set. Serve in the dishes as wobbly if turned out! Take out of fridge an hour before eating and serve with rolls or brown bread and butter.

AUBERGINES

When used in recipes like moussaka or lasagne it is a good idea, (healthier and easier) to steam the aubergines instead of frying them. They can be salted first to remove some of their bitterness, but it is important to wash the salt off.

AUBERGINES WITH TOMATOES

2 large aubergines, sliced
Oil for frying
1 clove garlic
Olive oil, l tsp sugar, pepper
1 lb (450g) ripe tomatoes, peeled and chopped
1 – 2 mozzarella cheeses, sliced
4 tbsp freshly grated parmesan
Basil or mint leaves, chopped

Make tomato sauce by frying garlic in 2 tablespoons olive oil. Add tomatoes, sugar, a little salt and pepper and herbs. Cook fast until reduced. Fry the aubergine slices either in shallow fat or in a deep fat pan. Drain on kitchen paper. Arrange the aubergine slices in a flat oval oven dish, cover with the tomato sauce and sprinkle with the cheeses. Bake in hot oven for at least 30 minutes.

This makes an excellent vegetarian meal if served with baked potato and a salad.

AVOCADO

Delicious if ripe and served simply with French dressing (see page 73). Allow half an avocado per person. Cut as late as possible and take a sliver off the outside so they stand square on the plate. Serve with a piece of lemon. Buy one or two extra in case any are black, in which case an avocado dip can be made.

See also: Tomato, avocado and mozzarella

AVOCADO DIP

One or two avocados
Juice of half a lemon
Salt and pepper
Small carton of double cream, crème fraîche or yoghourt
Green food colouring

Mash avocados and mix in other ingredients.

Serve with crudities – carrots, cubes of cucumber, sprigs of cauliflower, crisps, etc.

AVOCADO RING

2 ripe avocados
4 oz (110g) prawns
4 oz (110g) button mushrooms, sliced
5 fl oz (150 ml) chicken stock
1 tbsp Worcester sauce
½ tsp paprika, salt and pepper
5 fl oz (150 ml) mayonnaise
5 fl oz (150 ml) double cream
2 tbsp dressing made with lemon juice, vinegar and seasoning
1 tbsp gelatine, 1 tbsp sherry

Ring mould

Dissolve gelatine in a tablespoon of sherry and 2 tablespoons of water by heating over hot water in a ramekin dish.   Then add to the chicken stock and leave to cool.

Mash avocados and season with salt, pepper, Worcester sauce and paprika.   Pour in gelatine mixture, combine and leave to thicken.   Lightly whip the cream and fold into the mixture with the mayonnaise.   Pour into a wetted ring mould and allow to set.

Turn out and fill the centre with prawns and mushrooms tossed with the dressing.

AVOCADO SALAD

Avocado
Lettuce, watercress
Knob of lard or dripping
Streaky bacon
Clove garlic, crushed
Thick slices white bread for croutons – see page 57

French dressing, made with:
    Lemon juice
    Olive oil, salt, pepper
    Sugar, mustard

Slice avocado and mix with French dressing in bottom of a salad bowl, made with equal amounts of lemon juice and olive oil, adding sugar, mustard, salt and pepper to taste.   Cover with sliced lettuce – iceberg ideal – and watercress.   Fry bacon pieces in little fat.   Drain and then add crushed garlic to the bacon fat in the pan and add cubes of bread to make croutons.   Put bacon and croutons on top of salad.   Cover with cling foil and leave in fridge.

At the last moment, stir well to mix in the dressing.

AVOCADO SOUP

2 ripe avocados
1 tsp curry powder
Salt, pepper
5 fl oz (150 ml) double cream
1 pt (570 ml) white stock
2 tsp lemon juice, cayenne pepper
Chopped parsley, chives or other herb

Halve and peel the avocados. Cut up and put in mixer, or crush with wooden spoon, adding curry powder, seasoning and cream. Combine stock with lemon juice. Bring gently to the boil and carefully add a little to the avocado. Finally blend all together with the rest of the stock.

Chill and garnish with the chopped herbs. Serve hot or iced if (and when) there is a heat wave!

AVOCADO WITH PRAWNS (8 – 10)

2 large avocados
1 lb (450g) peeled prawns or 2 lb (1 kg) prawns in their shells*
3 oz (75g) walnuts
3 sticks celery, chopped

Dressing:
    10 fl oz (300 ml) mayonnaise
    1 tbsp horseradish cream
    2 tbsp tomato ketchup
    2 tbsp single cream
    Sherry, Worcester sauce

Freeze the shells for making stock or soup

Slice avocados and coat in lemon juice. Mix with the celery, walnuts and prawns. Make a dressing by mixing the rest of the ingredients together and add carefully to the avocado mixture.

Put in small attractive bowls on green salad leaves with a slice of lemon. My daughter and I invented this starter one Christmas when two of the avocados were black!

AVOCADO WITH WALNUTS (6)

3 ripe avocados
1 clove garlic, peeled and crushed
2 tbsp lemon juice
1 tsp Dijon mustard
Salt and pepper
4 fl oz (110 ml) olive oil
1 tbsp capers, chopped
3 oz (75g) chopped walnuts

Combine garlic, lemon juice, mustard, olive oil, capers, salt and pepper and shake in a bottle.

Place each peeled and halved avocado upside down on individual plates and cut into five lengthways Dribble the dressing over the avocados, garnish with the walnuts and serve.

BANANA YOGHOURT CREAM (6)

3 large bananas
10 fl oz (300 ml) plain yoghourt
7 fl oz (200 ml) double cream
Grated rind and juice ½ lemon
3 dsp brown sugar

Cut up the bananas, place in mixer or mash in a basin and add yoghourt, sugar and lemon juice and rind. Whip the cream and carefully add the banana mixture. Pour into ramekin dishes and leave in fridge or freeze. This should make about six. This is a useful way of using up left over cream and yoghourts and is very quick to make.

BARBECUE SAUCE

2 oz (50g) butter
1 onion, finely chopped
1 clove garlic, crushed
2 tbsp vinegar
7 fl oz (200 ml) water
1 tsp mustard, pinch cayenne
2 tbsp Demerara sugar
1 thick slice of lemon

Melt the butter and fry the chopped onion and the crushed garlic gently for 3 minutes. Stir in all the other ingredients, bring to the boil and simmer for 15 minutes.

   Add: 2 tbsp Worcester sauce
            6 tbsp tomato ketchup
            2 tbsp tomato puree
            Salt, pepper

Cook for another 5 minutes and finally remove the lemon. Serve hot or cold.

BEANS (FRENCH) ON TOAST

French beans
Mushroom soup (condensed)
Bread
Dripping or oil
Seasoning

Cook French beans and cut up if necessary. Reheat in a tin of mushroom soup. Meanwhile fry some bread and then top with the mushroom mixture. Season.

This was a recipe, which our German au pair girl used to make.

BEEF – BOILED

3 lb (1.4 kg) piece of lean brisket (not salted)*
1 – 2 tbsp beef dripping or oil
2 onions, sliced
2 carrots, sliced
2 stalks of celery, cut into sticks
salt, pepper
Parsley, thyme and bay leaf
5 fl oz (150 ml) stock

Silverside or topside could also be used for this recipe

Brown the beef on top of the stove in an ovenproof dish or saucepan.   Remove and brown the vegetables in the hot fat. Cover and cook for about 7 minutes.   Return the joint, add the herbs, seasonings and liquid. Cover and cook in a moderate oven for 1 to 2 hours.

Serve as a joint with Yorkshire pudding and gravy, drained from the vegetables, together with cabbage, Brussels sprouts or runner beans.

BEEF BOURGUIGNON (9 – 10)

3 lb (1.4 kg) chuck steak, cut into small pieces*
6 oz (175g) streaky smoked bacon, chopped
3 onions, sliced
3 tbsp oil
Thyme, parsley, bay leaf
8 fl oz (225 ml) red wine
12 fl oz (350 ml) beef stock
Clove of garlic, paprika
3 tbsp flour, 1 tbsp tomato puree
12 oz (325g) button mushrooms
12 oz (325g) button onions

* Marinade meat, if possible, overnight in red wine, with a slice of onion and carrot and ½ clove of garlic*

Fry meat well in the oil, add chopped bacon, sliced onions and a crushed clove of garlic. Cook very well (for about 15 minutes) and then stir in the flour, a pinch of paprika and a tablespoon of tomato puree. Cook for a few more minutes, add the liquid and stir while bringing to the boil. Add button vegetables and cook for either 1½ hours in a moderate oven or in a slow oven for 3 to 4 hours.

Serve with a salad and baked potato or rice.

BEEF CARBONADE (3 – 4)

1 lb (450g) skirt of beef
1 carrot, sliced
1 onion, sliced
1 green pepper, diced
5 fl oz (150 ml) beer and 5 fl oz (150 ml) beef stock
1 oz (25g) dripping, 1 tbsp flour

Topping:
    French bread
    Grated cheese
    Mustard

Cut beef into small pieces and cook in a casserole dish on top of the stove in dripping until brown. Add vegetables and continue cooking for about 5 minutes. Add a tablespoon of flour, cook for a few minutes more and then pour on the liquid, stirring until boiling. Cover and put in a cool to moderate oven and cook for about 3 hours until meat is very tender.

Half an hour before serving, remove lid and add slices of French bread, buttered both sides, but with the uppermost side also covered with mustard. Top with 2 handfuls of grated cheese and return to a moderate oven for half an hour or longer.

BEEF CASSEROLE (4)

2 oz (50g) margarine or butter
1½ lb (675g) chuck steak, cut into pieces
2 onions, peeled and chopped
Small tin of tomatoes
2 oz (50g) sultanas
1 tsp curry powder
Beef stock cube and 10 fl oz (300 ml) water
2 heaped tbsp flour
Pepper and salt

Place all ingredients in a large saucepan. Bring to the boil and simmer gently for 2 hours or transfer to a casserole dish and cook in a moderate oven for 2 – 3 hours with the lid on.

Serve with rice or baked potatoes.

This is the simplest of recipes, yet delicious.

BEEF EN CROUTE (8)

2½ lb (1.2 kg) beef fillet
Tbsp brandy
8 oz (225g) mushrooms
1 large onion
2 oz (50g) bacon
2 oz (50g) butter
Salt and black pepper
1 lb (450g) puff pastry (frozen or ready made)
1 egg yolk

Melt the butter and add chopped mushrooms, onion and bacon, finely chopped. Cook until butter is absorbed. Leave to cool.

Brush the beef with brandy, salt and pepper and roast for 20 minutes in a hot oven (220C/425F/ Gas 7).   Cool and cut into slices (2/3 per person) three-quarters of the way down.   Fill gaps with mushroom mixture.   Roll out the pastry, place meat on it and make a parcel joining at the top. Brush with beaten egg yolk and water sealing well.   Place on baking tin with small sides, decorate with pastry leaves and put in the fridge until needed.

Cook in a pre-heated hot oven (220C/425F/Gas 7) for 30 minutes until well browned.   Be sure to use a tin with sides otherwise you could set the oven alight with the hot fat!

BEEF FILLET – COLD (4 – 6)*

1½ – 2 lb (675g – 900g) piece of fillet beef
2 – 3 tbsp olive oil

Sauce: 4 tbsp olive oil, 1 tbsp sesame oil
       2 tbsp Kikkoman soy sauce
       2 tbsp balsamic vinegar
       1 tsp Dijon mustard, ½ tsp caster sugar

This is a very good recipe for a smart picnic. It needs to be made the day before.

Heat the oven to 200C/400F/Gas 6. Heat a heavy frying pan until very hot. Brush the piece of beef with olive oil and season. Fry in the pan and turn so that it browns all over. Transfer to the oven and roast for 25 minutes for medium rare. Remove from the oven and cover loosely with foil while it cools. Wrap tightly in cling film and leave in fridge overnight. The next day slice thinly and leave wrapped in the fridge.

Put all the ingredients for the sauce in a bottle and shake well to mix. Serve with the beef separately.

BEEF FILLET WITH MUSTARD SAUCE (6 – 8)

2½ lb (1.2 kg) beef fillet – thick end,
    with piece of fat tied over the top*
Knob of butter and tbsp olive oil

Mustard butter:
    4 oz (110g) butter
    Tsp English mustard
    Squeeze lemon juice
    Seasoning

Ask the butcher to do this

To make the mustard butter, cream the butter with a teaspoon of mustard, a little salt, a squeeze of lemon juice and some freshly ground black pepper. Make into a roll, wrap in foil and put in fridge.

Put the beef into a roasting tin with a knob of butter and tablespoon of olive oil in a pre-heated moderate oven (180C/350F/Gas 4) for 1 – 1 ½ hours, basting as much as possible.

Carve 2 slices each, with one slice of mustard butter.

BEEF – ROAST

2½ lb – 3½ lb (approx. 1.4 kg) joint – rolled ribs of beef
1 lb (450g) potatoes
1 lb (450g) parsnips
3 oz (75g) lard or dripping

For gravy:
    Tbsp flour
    Stock, wine and/or little crème fraîche
    Worcester sauce, seasoning

Par boil – for just 2 to 3 minutes – potatoes and parsnips. Drain. Put around the joint in the roasting tin with some fat.

2 hours before serving put in pre-heated oven – 180C/350F/Gas 4. Remove from the oven half to a quarter of an hour before the meal, and cook individual Yorkshire puddings in hot oven – 220C/425F/Gas 7. Do not cook in a fan oven. Place the joint on the serving dish and keep hot. Drain off some of the fat. Put the tin on the top of the stove to make the gravy. Sprinkle in a little flour. Cook till it browns, then pour on liquid (juice from the vegetables or water with some wine) a drop of Worcester sauce and some seasoning. Bring up to the boil and simmer before straining into a gravy boat.

Serve with horseradish sauce and mustard.

BEEF STEW WITH DUMPLINGS (4)

1½ lb (675g) leg of beef (stewing beef) cut into small pieces
1 carrot, sliced
1 onion, sliced
Beef stock cube with 1 pint (570 ml) water to cover
Dripping, lard or oil
1 heaped tbsp flour

Dumplings:
    4 oz (110g) self-raising flour or plain flour with tsp baking powder
    2 oz (50g) suet, tsp salt, 1 – 2 tbsp chopped parsley

Fry meat in fat or oil in a casserole on top of the stove for about 10 minutes and then add vegetables and cook for another 10 minutes. Add flour, cook for a minute or two, add the liquid and bring to the boil. Cook in moderate oven for about 2 – 3 hours with the lid on.

Make dumplings by mixing the ingredients together, adding a little water to make a stiff paste and rolling into about 12 balls and leaving in fridge until needed. 45 minutes before serving, remove lid and add dumplings – baste but leave on top of the dish.

Serve with potatoes and a vegetable.

BEEF STIR-FRY (4)

1 lb (450g) rump steaks*
3 tbsp soy sauce
1 leek, 1 carrot
4 oz (110g) mushrooms
Red pepper
1 inch piece of root ginger
3 tbsp sesame oil
4 oz (110g) bean sprouts

Try to buy cheaper off-cuts for this recipe

Remove beef from the fridge (it is easier to cut when cold) and cut into thin strips. Put in a bowl and pour over 3 tablespoons soy sauce. Mix well and leave to marinade for at least half an hour. Wash the leek and cut into strips, peel the carrot and cut into matchsticks, de-seed and chop the pepper carefully and slice the mushrooms. Peel the ginger and cut into very thin strips.

Heat the oil in a frying pan. Drain the beef and add to the pan, keeping back the marinade.
Stir fry for 3 minutes over a high heat. Remove and keep warm. Add the vegetables and ginger and stir-fry for 3 to 4 minutes. Return the beef, add the marinade and bean sprouts. Cook for 3 minutes and serve. Noodles are good with this dish.

BEEF STROGONOFF (8)

3 lb (1.4 kg) beef – rump steak or pieces of off-cut rump*
4 oz (110g) butter
4 onions
8 oz (225g) mushrooms
4 level tbsp flour
2 tbsp tomato puree
2 tsp English mustard
1 pt (570 ml) liquid (beef stock with red wine)
Small carton of sour cream

Ask a friendly butcher for this!

Cut beef into thin strips, season well and leave for 2 hours or longer if time allows. Fry sliced onions in butter, then add sliced mushrooms and fry for 3 minutes. Add the beef, stir well with a fork and cook for 6 minutes. Sprinkle with flour, cook for another 3 minutes, then add tomato puree, mustard and stock. Bring to the boil. Add the sour cream, put on lid and simmer gently for a quarter of an hour. Leave until needed.

Reheat on top of the stove, bringing to the boil again and adding seasoning if necessary.

Serve with rice and green salad.

BLACKBERRY CRUMBLE (6)

1 lb (450g) blackberries
2 lb (900g) apples
7 oz (200g) granulated sugar
1 lemon – rind and juice

Topping:
  6 oz (175g) plain flour
  6 oz (175g) caster sugar
  4 oz (110g) ground almonds
  8 oz (225g) butter

Peel, core and slice the apples and put in a soufflé or pie dish with the blackberries, the sugar and the rind and juice of a lemon.

Mix the flour, the caster sugar, ground almonds and butter in a mixer or by hand. Put on top of the fruit pressing it down well and marking it with a fork. Cook in a moderate oven for one hour.

Serve with pouring cream and be careful as this will be very hot when it comes out of the oven!

BLACKCURRANT FRANGIPANE

Pastry: 8 oz (225g) plain flour
2 tbsp icing sugar
5 oz (150g) butter
1 egg

Filling: 4 oz (110g) unsalted butter
4 oz (110g) caster sugar
2 eggs
4 oz (110g) ground almonds
2 tbsp self-raising flour

Glaze: ½ jar apricot jam
Juice of ½ lemon
2 tbsp brandy (or water)

Fruit: 1 lb (450g) blackcurrants or mixture of soft fruits

Mix pastry in mixer and leave in fridge.   Roll out into a large fluted flan dish.   Line with foil and baking beans.   Bake in a moderate oven for at least 30 minutes.   Remove from the oven and spread apricot jam thinly over the base.

Mix butter and sugar together and add eggs, flour and ground almonds. Spread onto flan and push fruit evenly into the mixture. Bake moderate oven for 30 minutes or longer until set (test with knife).   Dust with caster sugar and return to the oven for another 5 minutes or so.   Remove from the oven and spoon over apricot glaze made by mixing the jam with lemon juice and brandy. Remaining glaze will keep in jam jar in fridge.

Leave to cool.   Serve with thick cream. This freezes well, but needs to be reheated briefly when it comes out of the freezer.

BLACKCURRANT WHIP (6)

Small tin or jar of blackcurrants
Small tin of evaporated milk
Blackcurrant jelly
5 fl oz (150 ml) Ribena

Put the tin of evaporated milk in the freezer or fridge to cool.   Melt the jelly with 5 fl oz (150 ml) water. Strain the juice from the blackcurrants and add to the jelly with the Ribena.   Put in the fridge to cool.   Beat the evaporated milk and pour in the cold jelly and continue beating until thick and mousse-like.   Pour into 6 individual glasses and leave to set in the fridge.   When starting to set distribute the blackcurrants over the top.   Return to fridge, but remove about an hour before serving to avoid a "gelatine" taste.

This is a recipe from my mother's collection that I can remember my grandmother making.

BLINIS (makes about 12 large ones)

3 oz (75g) strong white flour
3 oz (75g) buckwheat flour
5 fl oz (150 ml) milk
½ oz (10g) fresh yeast (or packet of dried)
2 eggs
3 fl oz (90 ml) sour cream

To serve: 4 slices smoked salmon
              ½ pt (300 ml) crème fraîche

Blini pan (optional)*

These are fun to use especially if you have two going at once!

Put the flours with a pinch of salt into a large bowl. Heat the milk and pour it onto the yeast. Separate the eggs and add the yolks and the sour cream to the milk and yeast and whisk. Pour this mixture into the flour stirring well making a batter. Cover and leave in a warm place to rise – about an hour.

Whisk the egg whites until soft and fold into the batter. Cover again and leave for about another hour until well risen. Heat a heavy pan with butter and cook the blinis, a tablespoon at a time, turning over when set. Or cook a teaspoon of the batter at a time to make miniature blinis.

To serve spread with crème fraîche and smoked salmon. These can be frozen and reheated at a later date.

BOMBE WITH CHOCOLATE*

Meringue:
    4 egg whites
    8 oz (225g) caster sugar

10 fl oz (300 ml) double cream
Brandy, Grand Marnier or other liqueur
6 oz (175g) dark chocolate

This bombe is also good on its own without the chocolate – served with fruit

Make meringues by beating the egg whites until stiff, adding half of the sugar and continuing to beat until really stiff. Fold in the rest of the sugar. Pile in rough spoonfuls onto a baking tray lined with non-stick parchment paper. Cook low oven for at least an hour until dry. Whip cream, add liqueur and broken pieces of meringue. Put into a rectangular box with lid or ice cream carton and put in the freezer.

The day it is to be eaten, melt chocolate with 6 tablespoons water over hot water and pour over the frozen bombe. Return to freezer. Turn onto a plate and leave in fridge before serving.

BRANDY BUTTER

8 oz (225g) unsalted butter
6 oz (175g) icing sugar
3 tbsp brandy
Grated peel of 1 orange

Put butter and icing sugar in mixer or a bowl. Mix well and then add brandy slowly. Add grated peel of one orange. Put in jar and keep in fridge.

Serve with Christmas pudding or mince pies.

BREAD BASES FOR CANAPES

Sliced bread
Butter – soft

Small cutter – 1 ¾" (4 cm)
2 or 3 miniature tart tins

Roll slices of bread with rolling pin to thin them. Cut into rounds with the pastry cutter. Put half on a baking sheet as they are. The other half, butter on both sides and press into miniature tart tins. If possible put another tin on the top to press the bread down.

Bake in oven 150C/300F/Gas 2 for about 20 minutes for the flat toasts and longer – for about 40 mins – for the little tarts.   Cool and keep in an airtight tin.

When needed top with hummus, tapenade, liver pate etc.

BREAD ROLLS (24)

1 lb (450g) strong flour
Pinch of salt
10 fl oz (300 ml) milk
1 egg
1 oz (25g) fresh yeast*
2 tbsp cooking oil
1 dsp sugar
Sesame or poppy seeds (optional)

Fresh yeast can be bought from the bread counter in some supermarkets or bakeries

Heat milk with sugar. Add little to yeast and leave till frothy. Put flour into mixer and add all liquid ingredients together and pour slowly onto the flour. Process for 30 seconds.   Leave to rise. Make into 24 rolls, either plain or twisted shapes. Leave to rise again, brush with milk and/or beaten egg and, if liked, shake on some sesame seeds or poppy seeds.   Bake in hot oven for 15 to 20 minutes until brown and easily removable from the baking sheet.   Keep in freezer.

BREAD SAUCE

10 fl oz (300 ml) milk
2 oz (50g) butter
1 small onion, chopped
1 small clove garlic, crushed
Bay leaf, 2 cloves
Blade of mace
Tsp dried sage
3 oz (75g) fresh white breadcrumbs
5 fl oz (150 ml) single cream
Seasoning – salt, pepper, grated nutmeg

Put milk in thick saucepan with all the flavourings and the butter and heat until hot. Add the breadcrumbs and cook until quite thick and smooth. Remove bay leaf, mace and cloves; add cream and adjust the seasoning.

Reheat in a double saucepan, with a buttered paper and lid, or in an ordinary saucepan, in which case a little more milk and a knob of butter will have to be added.

This can be frozen and reheated. Serve with roast chicken and roast turkey.

BRETON CAKE

Topping:
    1 oz (25g) butter
    1 oz (25g) self-raising flour
    2 oz (50g) soft brown sugar

8 oz (250g) self-raising flour
½ tsp baking powder
3 oz (75g) butter
3 oz (75g) caster sugar
1 large egg
5 fl oz (150 ml) milk

8" spring form cake tin

Set the oven to 190C/375F/Gas 5. Melt the butter for the topping. Leave to cool and mix together the flour and soft brown sugar, ready to mix in with the butter.

Put the flour and baking powder for the cake in a mixer. Mix in the butter and sugar. Pour in the egg and milk. Turn on the mixer briefly to form a batter. Pour into the greased cake tin and spread level. Quickly add the topping mixture to the melted butter and fork over the top of the cake. Put in the pre-heated oven and cook for 40 minutes or longer. It is ready when a skewer comes out clean. Cool in the tin for about ten minutes and then leave on a wire rack.

BRIOCHE

¼ oz (5g) fresh yeast* mixed with 2 tbsp warm milk
10 oz (275g) strong flour
Tsp salt
Tbsp sugar
3 eggs, lightly beaten
6 oz (175g) butter, melted and cooled

Beaten egg to glaze

Fresh yeast can be bought from the bread counter of some supermarkets or bakeries

Mix yeast with the milk and leave until frothy. Sift flour and salt into a bowl with the sugar. Make well in centre and pour in eggs, then yeast mixture and butter. Work in flour to give a soft, sticky dough. Cover with cling film and leave to rise in a warm place for about 1 – 2 hours until double in size. Knock down, cover and leave for at least another hour.

Either put into buttered loaf tin or make individual buns (with small ball on top) placed in muffin-type tins. Cover and leave till well risen. Brush with egg wash and bake in a hot oven for about 10 minutes until they turn out of the tins easily.

I always make these in my magimix and they turn out all right.

BUTTERSCOTCH WHIP*

1 large (410g) tin chilled evaporated milk
2 – 3 drops vanilla extract
1 oz (25g) butter or margarine
3 oz (75g) Demerara sugar
1 packet of gelatine
2 tbsp sherry

At the moment this is my grandchildren's favourite pudding!

Put milk in a large mixing bowl with two to three drops of vanilla extract. Put butter in a saucepan over low heat. Put gelatine in a ramekin dish with 2 tablespoons of sherry. Place the ramekin dish in a small saucepan with a little water over a low heat to melt. Start whipping the milk and then add 3 oz Demerara sugar to the melted butter in the saucepan. Stir and cook for 1 minute. Continue beating milk and add first the cooled melted gelatine and then the butter and sugar mixture, beating hard all the time. Quickly pour into glass bowl when well mixed and place immediately in the fridge to set.

Remove from refrigerator about an hour before serving.

CABBAGE – BRAISED

1 small firm green cabbage
6 oz (175g) bacon slices
6 oz (175g) button onions or shallots
2 oz (50g) butter, 2 tbsp oil
1 clove crushed garlic
2 fl oz (50 ml) dry white wine
Salt and pepper

Remove core from cabbage and shred finely. Rinse and drain. Cut bacon into thin strips. Put in saucepan with cold water and bring to boil.   Drain and dry.

In ovenproof casserole, which goes on top of stove, cook bacon and onions in the fat until brown. Then stir in garlic and cabbage and cook for another minute. Add the wine and seasoning.   Cover and cook in moderate oven for about 40 minutes.

CARROTS

Carrots can be plainly cooked, sliced in water or steamed.   However "Vichy Carrots" are delicious, but you do have to be careful not to burn them. If the carrots are large, slice into quarters; if small, leave whole. Cover (just) with water, a nut of butter, pinch of salt and a teaspoon of sugar. Simmer slowly until all the water has evaporated and the carrots are glazed.

You can also make a carrot puree by steaming sliced carrots, putting them in a blender with a nut of butter, a tablespoon of cream, salt and pepper.   Mix well and put into oven dish or individual dishes. Cover with foil and reheat.

CARROT AND LEEK SOUP

12 oz (325g) carrots
2 leeks
15 fl oz (450 ml) stock
5 fl oz (150 ml) milk
2 oz (50g) butter
salt, pepper
6 tbsp single cream

Melt the butter and fry sliced carrots and leeks for 5 – 10 minutes.   Add the stock and seasoning and simmer for 15 minutes.   Liquidise or sieve.   Add milk and cream.   Reheat and taste, adding more seasoning if necessary.

This is a simple soup, not as sophisticated as carrot and orange soup, but just as good.

CARROT AND ORANGE SOUP

1 lb (450g) new carrots
1 onion
1 oz (25g) butter
2 pints (1.1 litre) chicken stock
Juice of 4 oranges
5 fl oz (150 ml) single cream
Tsp sugar, salt
Chopped chives or other herbs

Scrape the carrots and slice, together with the onion.   Melt the butter in large saucepan and fry carrots and onions gently for a few minutes. Pour on the stock, seasoning and sugar, bring to the boil and simmer with lid on for one hour. Liquidise or sieve, add the juice of the oranges and then add the cream very slowly.   Heat or serve chilled. Top with snipped chives.   Served chilled, this is delicious for a luncheon or dinner party with hot rolls.

If in a hurry you can make this soup using a tin of carrots and a small can of orange juice.

CAULIFLOWER CHEESE WITH BACON (4)*

1 medium cauliflower
1½ oz (30g) butter
1½ oz (30g) flour
¾ pt (450 ml) milk
Tsp mustard, salt, grated pepper and nutmeg
6 oz (175g) Cheddar cheese, grated
8 slices smoked streaky bacon
8 slices cooked potato

A good all-in-one supper dish, which can be made ahead.

Break cauliflower into florets and steam until soft – about 15 mins. Meanwhile make a white sauce. Melt the butter in a small saucepan. Mix in the flour, stir and cook for a minute. Add the milk, mustard, a little salt, ground pepper and nutmeg. Stir well and bring to the boil. Then turn down the heat and add the grated Cheddar cheese.

Put the cauliflower into a large soufflé type dish. Pour over the sauce. Add the slices of bacon (rolled up) and potato to the top.   Bake in a moderate oven for up to an hour.

CELERIAC

The easiest way of cooking celeriac is to peel off the hard skin and cut it into chip-like pieces. Boil for about 20 minutes. Drain and put into flat ovenproof dish with butter and chopped parsley. Reheat in a moderate oven.

Celeriac puree can be made by boiling celeriac pieces until soft and then mashing and mixing them with an equal amount of mashed potatoes, with plenty of seasoning and a little butter.

CELERIAC CHIPS

Large celeriac
Frying oil*
Deep fat basket
Sugar thermometer

Any oil can be used but grapeseed oil is excellent for frying

Half fill a deep fat basket with frying oil. Heat to a temperature of 175C (caramel) using a sugar thermometer. Peel the celeriac and slice thinly. Fry in small quantities, separating with a fork and draining on kitchen paper when brown. Leave to cool.

Transfer to a flat ovenproof dish and reheat in a low to moderate oven.

These are delicious with all game dishes. Parsnip chips can be made in the same way.

CELERY – BRAISED

The easiest way to cook celery is to wash it and cut it into small pieces. Place a spoonful of oil and a knob of butter into a small thick saucepan. Put in the celery pieces and stew (covered with a buttered paper and the lid) for about 20 minutes. Then transfer to a flat ovenproof dish and top with some grated Parmesan cheese and seasoning. Cover with foil.

Cook when needed for about 30 minutes.

Good with game or pheasant and a useful way of using up pieces of celery.

CHARLOTTE RUSSE

Raspberry jelly with 15 fl oz (450 ml) water, including 1 tbsp Crème de Cassis
10 fl oz (300 ml) double cream
6 small sheets (½ oz or 10g) leaf gelatine
5 fl oz (150 ml) milk, dsp caster sugar
Tbsp sherry (or brandy)
Vanilla extract
Sponge fingers
Cherries and angelica to decorate

Wet small soufflé dish or 6 inch (15 cm) cake tin.   Make the jelly and put a thin layer in the dish.
When starting to set, decorate the base with halved glacé cherries and diamonds of angelica and
cover with a thin layer of the jelly. Leave till starting to set, then add more jelly to depth of half an
inch.   Leave for a little while, then push sponge fingers into the jelly all round the outside of the
dish. Dissolve the gelatine and sugar in the milk, add a tablespoon of sherry slowly and a few drops
of vanilla extract. Whip the cream and when it has cooled, stir in the gelatine mixture. Pour on top
of the set jelly and keep in the fridge.

To serve, turn out carefully onto an attractive dish. If necessary dip the base quickly in hot water.
This is an old-fashioned recipe – one of my mother's favourites.

CHEESE AND PINEAPPLE SALAD

Small fresh pineapple
8 oz (225g) Cheddar cheese
Lettuce, cucumber
Apple – crisp type (e.g. Braeburn)
Handful of nuts – almonds or walnuts

Peel and core pineapple and cut into pieces. Cube the cheese and cucumber, having removed the
skin and seeds.   Slice the apple without removing the skin. Mix all together with the nuts. Put
lettuce in salad bowl and cover with all the ingredients. Serve with rolls and Melba toast.

CHEESE BISCUITS

4 oz (110g) wholemeal flour
2 oz (50g) medium oatmeal, pinch of salt
3 oz (75g) soft margarine
3 oz (75g) Cheddar cheese, grated
Bunch of parsley or coriander, chopped

Mix flour, oatmeal, salt and margarine together. Add grated cheese and finely chopped parsley
or coriander.   Turn on to floured slab, roll out and cut into small rounds.   Bake on greased baking
trays and cook in a moderate oven for 10 – 20 minutes.   Leave biscuits on tray for a short while,
then transfer to wire rack. Keep in an airtight tin.   Delicious with cheese and useful to serve with
drinks. They are unusual and definitely worth making – they are not much trouble.

CHEESE FILOS

8 oz (225g) feta cheese*
8 oz (225g) curd cheese
Bunch of spring onions
1 egg
4 oz (110g) butter
Salt, pepper
1 packet of filo pastry

Try to buy cubed feta cheese, sold in glass jars in oil

Remove filo pastry if necessary from deep freeze and cover with a cloth. Trim the spring onions and chop. Mix egg and curd cheese, add seasoning and cubed feta cheese and the onions.

Melt the butter and taking one sheet of filo at a time cut it into 9 inch (23 cm) squares. Brush with melted butter, fold over and brush again. Place a tablespoon of the filling ½ inch from bottom left and fold over 3 times making a triangle enclosing the cheese filling. Brush with butter and press down sides. Put in fridge. About 15 minutes before eating bake in hot to moderate oven till crisp. Eat hot with salad as a supper dish. Any left over can be frozen and reheated.

Miniature puffs (to serve with drinks) can be made with any left over filo pastry.

CHEESE PUDDING

1 oz (25g) butter
1 pint (570 ml) milk
4 oz (110g) fine white breadcrumbs
4 oz (110g) grated Cheddar cheese
2 eggs
Salt, pepper, dry mustard

Heat milk with the butter. Mix together the breadcrumbs, the grated cheese and the seasonings. Pour hot (not boiling) milk over the dry ingredients. Separate the eggs, beat the egg yolks and add to the mixture. Whip egg whites and fold in lightly. Pour into a pie dish and leave to stand for 30 minutes. Bake in moderate oven for 40 – 50 minutes until firm and golden brown.

This serves two as a supper dish – with a salad.

CHEESE PUFFS

3½ oz (85g) butter
9 fl oz (260 ml) liquid, half milk and half water
Tsp salt, ground black pepper
5 oz (150g) plain white flour, sifted
4 small eggs
3 oz (75g) Gruyere and Parmesan cheese, grated and mixed

Put butter, liquid and salt in saucepan. Melt butter and then bring mixture to boil. Boil for 30 seconds, stirring with wooden spoon. Remove from heat and tip in all flour at once. Return to the heat for a minute and beat until smooth. Remove and put in bowl. Beat in eggs one at a time until shiny. Add cheeses and pepper. Pre-heat oven to 220C/425F/Gas 6. Line a baking sheet with non-stick parchment paper and pipe out balls using ½ inch nozzle, or put out in spoonfuls. Dust with cayenne or paprika. Makes about 30 small puffs. Bake for about 5 minutes, then open oven door a little and bake for about another 10 minutes until brown and crisp. Serve with drinks.

These can be frozen and reheated from frozen. Any left over can be used with soups.

CHEESE SOUFFLÉ (4)

1 oz (25g) butter
1 oz (25g) flour
10 fl oz (300 ml) milk
4 eggs
2 oz (50g) Cheddar cheese
2 oz (50g) Parmesan
3 tbsp chopped fresh parsley
Salt, pepper and little mustard

Prepare 4 ovenproof bowls or a soufflé dish by buttering and coating with breadcrumbs. Melt butter, add flour, cook a little, and pour on milk stirring well until boiling. Remove from the heat and leave till cold. Separate the eggs and stir in the egg yolks, mixing well. Then add grated cheeses, seasoning and herbs. Beat egg whites, stir a tablespoon into the cheese mixture and then fold in the rest. Pour into prepared bowls and bake in pre-heated moderate oven for about 30 minutes until puffed up and golden. Serve at once.

Alternatively, this can be made in advance (surprisingly even up to the inclusion of the egg whites) and left in the fridge. Put in the oven 30 minutes or longer before ready to eat.

CHESTNUTS

These are a nightmare to peel and in my opinion not worth the trouble, as you can now buy them whole and already peeled, either in tins or dried. You can, of course, also buy tins of sweetened or unsweetened chestnut puree, which are very good.

CHESTNUT LOG

1 large tin of sweetened chestnut puree or
   1 tin of unsweetened with 4 oz (110g) icing sugar and tsp vanilla extract
4 oz (110g) unsalted butter
5 oz (150g) dark chocolate
1 tbsp brandy

Meringues:
   2 egg whites
   4 oz (110g) caster sugar

Make meringues by whipping the egg whites (not too fresh) until stiff. Add half of the sugar, a tablespoon at a time and continue beating until very stiff. Fold in the rest of the sugar, using a metal spoon. Put out in rough heaps on a baking tray and cook in a low oven until crisp and dry. Remove from the tin and leave to cool. Melt butter and chocolate over hot water. Do not allow the chocolate to get too hot. Add chestnut puree and mix well. Break meringues into pieces and add to the puree together with a tablespoon of brandy. Line a thin oblong tin with foil. Pour the mixture into it. Smooth top and cover with the foil. Put in freezer.

To serve, put on a long plate, decorate and replace in freezer until just before starting to eat. This is rather rich so serve in thin slices with pouring cream.

CHESTNUT STUFFING

Packet of dried chestnuts, soaked overnight in cold water or
   tin or packet of whole peeled chestnuts*
8 oz (225g) streaky bacon
2 oz (50g) butter
4 oz (110g) fresh brown breadcrumbs
1 egg
1 bunch watercress
Tbsp caster sugar
2 tsp salt, ground black pepper.

It is not worth making chestnut stuffing with unpeeled chestnuts as it takes too long!

Drain the chestnuts and cut in half. Chop the bacon and fry slowly. Add the chestnuts, increase heat and fry quickly. Remove with slotted spoon. Add butter to the bacon in the pan and fry breadcrumbs until brown. Add to the chestnuts with plenty of seasoning, tbsp sugar, the chopped watercress and the beaten egg.

This is enough stuffing for the body of a 14 – 16 lb turkey.

CHICKEN

See also: Coq au vin
Poulet en cocotte
Thai chicken curry
Vol-au-vent

CHICKEN CASSEROLE (4)

4 chicken joints
8 chipolata sausages
4 oz (110g) bacon rashers or pieces
Onions, carrots and mushrooms as available
1 pt (570 ml) liquid – stock, wine etc.
Tbsp tomato puree and tbsp flour
Herbs, such as parsley, thyme and/or tarragon
Knob of butter and tbsp oil
Garlic and seasoning

Fry chicken pieces in butter and oil in an ovenproof dish, which also goes on top of the stove.
Remove chicken and fry sliced vegetables, sausages and pieces of bacon.   Add a tablespoon of
flour, tomato puree and liquid.   Bring to the boil and return the pieces of chicken.   Put the
casserole into a moderate oven and cook for at least an hour. Baked potatoes are good with this.

CHICKEN – CHINESE STYLE (4)

4 chicken breasts
4 leeks
2 – 3 tbsp vegetable oil
Marinade: 2 tbsp cornflour
2 tbsp soy sauce
2 tbsp brandy
2 tsp ginger, tsp sugar
Sauce: Tsp flour, 2 tsp soy sauce
5 fl oz (150 ml) chicken stock or water + ½ cube
Noodles, sesame oil

Mix marinade ingredients together and pour over chicken, cut into small pieces. Leave for at least
half an hour. Make sauce by mixing together the flour and soy sauce and the stock.   Slice the leeks
thinly and wash and drain.

Heat a tablespoon of vegetable oil in a sauté pan and cook the chicken breasts, drained from the
marinade, for a minute. Remove with a slotted spoon and put in a dish in the oven to keep hot.
Add more oil and cook leeks for 4 minutes.   Return chicken to the pan and pour on the thickened
chicken stock.   Bring to the boil and then serve with noodles – cooked for 4 minutes – and tossed
in sesame oil.

This recipe was given to us by a Swiss friend in Geneva.   An excellent very quick meal.

CHICKEN DRUMSTICKS

8 chicken drumsticks
2 tbsp oil
Tbsp runny honey
Tbsp soy sauce*
Herbs, chopped
Salt, ground pepper

Foil

Kikkoman soy sauce is one of the best

Mix the liquid ingredients together and add chopped herbs, as available, and some seasoning. Marinade the drumsticks in this sauce.

Wrap each drumstick in a foil parcel including a little of the sauce. Bake in a moderate oven for 40 minutes in a shallow roasting tin. Remove from the oven. Take off the foil and serve at once or keep in the foil for a barbecue or picnic.

CHICKEN IN BARBECUE SAUCE

Chicken joints or thighs and/or breasts
Oil for frying

Sauce:
    1 tbsp oil
    2 tbsp chopped chives
    3 tbsp soft brown sugar
    2 tsp tomato ketchup
    3 tsp French mustard
    1 tsp black pepper
    Tin of tomatoes or 1 lb (450g) ripe tomatoes, skinned and chopped.

Fry chicken in oil until brown and place in a casserole dish. Fry the chives in oil in a large saucepan and add the rest of the sauce ingredients. Stir well and cook for about 10 minutes. Pour over the chicken in the casserole, cover and bake in a moderate to hot oven for one hour or longer.

Serve with baked potatoes and a green salad.

This was one of my mother's favourite recipes.

CHICKEN PROVENCALE

Chicken breasts – one per person (no more than six for this sauce)
2 cloves garlic, sliced thinly
Lemon juice, salt and pepper
2 tbsp olive oil

Sauce:
    2 tbsp olive oil, 8 cloves chopped garlic
    12 sprigs thyme, 6 basil leaves, 2 sprigs marjoram
    8 anchovy fillets, chopped, 24 black olives, pitted
    1 tin (400g) tomatoes
    ¼ bottle dry white wine

Make the sauce by heating the oil and cooking the garlic and herbs for 5 minutes.   Add the rest of the sauce ingredients and simmer for 15 minutes. With a sharp knife make slits in the chicken flesh. Push thin slivers of garlic into the slits.   Rub skin with lemon juice and season with salt and pepper. Heat oil in ovenproof dish with flameproof base and brown chicken.

Pour over the sauce, cover with foil or lid and bake in a hot oven for about 30 minutes.   Serve with rice and a salad, such as chicory, watercress and orange.

CHICKEN – ROAST

Chicken – 3½ lb (1.6 kg)
1 lb (450g) chipolata sausages
3 – 4 rashers streaky bacon
Onion, lemon, butter
French tarragon and/or other herbs
1 oz (25g) dripping or lard
1 lb (450g) potatoes

Place chicken in roasting tin on a grid. Put an onion, half a lemon and herbs (tarragon if available) inside chicken. Put 3 – 4 rashers of bacon on the breast.   Add dripping or lard to the pan.   Bring some potatoes to the boil and cook for a few minutes only. Drain and put round the chicken.

Put chicken in hot oven (200C/400F/Gas 6) for 1½ hours.   Add the sausages to the chicken and potatoes half an hour into the cooking time and baste the chicken and turn the potatoes. Put chicken, potatoes and sausages on serving dishes, having removed stuffing from the chicken. Keep hot while making gravy. When making gravy, stir a small amount of flour into the fat, mix well and cook until brown and then pour in some vegetable water and/or stock, wine etc. Bring to boil and strain into a gravy boat. Gravy should be thin and lightly seasoned.

CHICKEN SALAD

8 oz (225g) cooked chicken
3 slices fresh pineapple

Mayonnaise:
   2 eggs
   1½ tbsp wine vinegar
   Salt and pepper
   10 fl oz (300 ml) oil – mixture of olive and groundnut or grapeseed
   Tbsp curry powder

Make mayonnaise in mixer or basin by mixing the vinegar, eggs and seasonings and then adding the oil drop by drop at first until it starts to thicken after which it can be poured in very slowly. Add a tablespoon of curry powder to taste.

Add this to pieces of cooked chicken and a few pieces of fresh pineapple. Leave covered until needed.

To save time bottled mayonnaise and tinned pineapple can be used but it won't be so good.

CHICKEN THIGHS

2 chicken thighs per person
2 oz (50g) butter
2 tbsp runny honey
2 tsp English mustard
2 tsp turmeric
Tsp curry powder
Salt and pepper

Sauce:
   2 tbsp plain yoghourt
   4 tbsp single cream
   2 tbsp chopped coriander
   1 tbsp parsley

Melt butter in frying pan. Add the honey, mustard, turmeric, curry powder and seasoning and stir till mixed. Remove from heat. Remove skin and bone from thighs and cut in half. Roll in the mixture to coat and place in a shallow ovenproof dish. Cover with foil. Bake in moderate to hot pre-heated oven for 30 to 40 minutes.

Mix together the yoghourt, single cream and chopped coriander and parsley and serve with the chicken, together with some plainly cooked noodles.

This is a very quick and easy dish, which can be prepared ahead.

CHICKEN THIGHS – STUFFED*

8 boned chicken thighs
Large packet of Philadelphia cream cheese
Handful of spinach leaves
8 or more dried apricots
8 or more slices of streaky bacon
Seasoning

Cocktail sticks

Served cold in slices this is a good unusual dish for a buffet party

Lay the thighs out flat and spread with the cheese. Cover each with a spinach leaf and put two halves of dried apricots on the top. Season and roll up as tightly as possible, at the same time, winding a slice of bacon round the chicken. Fix with one or two cocktail sticks. Place on a baking sheet with low sides.

Bake in a moderate to hot oven for about 30 to 40 minutes. Remove the cocktail sticks. Eat some with vegetables and leave some to cool. When cold cut into slices and eat with salads.

CHICORY, WATERCRESS AND ORANGE SALAD (6 – 8)

3 oranges
2 large bags or bunches of watercress
1 pack (2 – 3 heads) red chicory
Handful of walnuts
Tbsp olive oil, tbsp lemon juice
Salt and pepper

Peel the oranges and cut into segments. Put into a large salad bowl with the rest of the ingredients. Mix the oil with the lemon juice and seasoning and pour over at the last moment.

CHILLI CON CARNE (3 – 4)

1 lb (450g) best minced beef
Tin kidney beans
2 tbsp oil
2 onions, finely chopped
3 small red chillies, without seeds and very finely chopped or
   1 tsp chilli powder and 1 tsp paprika
5 fl oz (150 ml) liquid (stock, tomato sauce and little liquid from bean tin)

Cook onions, without browning, in large saucepan, add spices, cook a little and add mince, stirring for 4 to 5 minutes until brown, then add beans and stock etc. Cover and cook on top of stove, if in a hurry, or cook for about 1½ hours in moderate oven. Serve with rice. Can be frozen.

CHOCOLATE APPLES

2 lb (900g) cooking apples, sliced
6 oz (175g) breadcrumbs
6 oz (175g) brown sugar
1 oz (25g) chocolate powder
4 oz (110g) butter

Melt butter and fry breadcrumbs. Add chocolate powder and sugar. Mix well. Place a layer of this mixture on the bottom of a soufflé dish. Cover with a layer of sliced apples. Continue layering breadcrumb mixture with the apples, finishing with a deep layer of the chocolate breadcrumbs.

Press down well and bake in a moderate oven for about an hour. This can be served hot, but we always eat it cold with thick cream.

CHOCOLATE CAKE

6 oz (175g) self raising flour
1½ tsp baking powder
6 oz (175g) caster or vanilla sugar
6 oz (175g) soft margarine
2 tbsp cocoa powder mixed with 3 tbsp boiling water
3 eggs
Filling:
    4 oz (120g) icing sugar
    1 oz (25g) chocolate powder
    2 oz (50g) butter
    3 oz (75g) caster sugar
    3 tbsp water

2 x 8" (20 cm) sandwich tins

Turn oven on to 180C/350F/Gas 4 and grease and line two 8 inch sandwich tins. Put all ingredients in mixer. Turn on briefly and then pour into tins. Cook approx. 25 minutes – until skewer comes out clean. Turn out and leave to cool.

While cake is cooking, make the filling by putting the icing sugar and chocolate powder in the mixer. Put the butter, caster sugar and water in a small saucepan and stir over heat until the sugar has dissolved and the butter has melted. Bring up to the boil and pour into the mixer. Mix and leave to cool a little.

Fill the cake with this and also put some on the top. Dust with icing sugar or decorate with crystallized violets or chocolate leaves.

CHOCOLATE CARAMEL SHORTBREAD

Shortbread:
  6 oz (175g) butter
  3 oz (75g) caster sugar
  9 oz (250g) plain flour
Caramel:
  6 oz (175g) unsalted butter
  3 oz (75g) caster sugar
  3 tbsp golden syrup
  7 oz (200g) sweetened condensed milk
Chocolate topping:
  6 oz (175g) dark chocolate
  2 oz (50g) unsalted butter

Tin with shallow sides, approx 8" x 12" (20 cm x 30 cm)

Mix the sugar, flour and pieces of butter for the shortbread in a mixer or by hand. Pat it out into a greased oblong tin and bake (180C/350F/Gas 4) for 20 – 30 mins. until brown. Leave to cool.

Place caramel ingredients into a saucepan and stir occasionally on a low heat until dissolved. Raise the heat and then stir continuously for five minutes or longer until the mixture changes to a caramel colour. Spread over the shortbread and leave to cool.

Melt chocolate and butter over a low heat. Pour over the caramel and spread into the corners. Mark when cooling and when set cut into squares. Keep in an airtight tin.

CHOCOLATE COOKIES

8 oz (225g) butter (or soft margarine)
5 oz (150g) soft brown sugar
Few drops vanilla extract
8 oz (225g) plain flour
½ tsp baking powder
2 tbsp cocoa powder
1 egg
Small packet chocolate chips
4 oz (110g) chopped walnuts

Beat fat and sugar together in mixer or by hand. Add extract, flour, baking powder and cocoa powder and egg and mix well. Add the chocolate chips and walnuts and mix all together. Put small spoonfuls on greased baking sheets leaving gaps between. Makes about 40. Cook in a moderate oven (180C/350F/Gas 4) for about 15 minutes. Remove and leave to cool. Freeze some and eat some.

CHOCOLATE CREPES (makes about 16)

5 oz (150g) plain flour, pinch salt
2 oz (50g) cocoa powder
2 oz (50g) caster sugar
14 fl oz (400 ml) milk
2 eggs
4 fl oz (100 ml) cream

Small omelette or crepe pan

Fillings: ¼ pt double cream, whipped, with 2 tbsp. Crème de Menthe liqueur
                ¼ pt double cream, whipped, with tbsp brandy and chestnut cream
                   from a small tin or tube

To freeze: Sheets of polythene tissue paper*

* *These are obtainable as Easy-Leave Sheets by mail order*

Sift the flour, cocoa, salt and sugar into a bowl and make a gap in the middle. Pour in one-third of the milk and the eggs into the middle and work into the powder with a wooden spoon to make a batter. Beat well and then stir in the cream and the rest of the milk. Sieve into a jug and leave for half an hour or longer.

Heat the pan with butter until very hot. Pour in a tablespoon of the mixture and swirl the pan to cover the base. The mixture should be like thin cream, so add more milk if necessary. When the crepe is set, use a spatula to turn it to cook the other side.   Repeat and stack until the mixture is finished.   Reheat over hot water and serve with caster sugar and one of the flavoured creams.

Any pancakes not needed, can be frozen between easy leave sheets in a polythene bag.

CHOCOLATE FUDGE

10 oz (275g) granulated sugar
2 oz (50g) dark chocolate
5 fl oz (150 ml) milk
2 oz (50g) unsalted butter

Oil a square tin. Put chocolate bits, sugar and milk in a medium sized saucepan.   Place pan on a low heat and stir until chocolate has melted and sugar dissolved. Increase heat and stir until boiling.   Reduce to moderate and boil for 5 minutes stirring occasionally. Test for soft ball, by putting a teaspoon of the mixture in cold water and seeing if it forms a ball. Remove from heat and leave for 5 minutes.   Add butter little by little and stir until melted and smooth. Pour into tin. Leave for 10 minutes.   Mark into squares and leave till really hard and set.   Cut, put into paper cases and store in airtight container.

This is an easy fudge, well worth making.

CHOCOLATE GATEAU

4 eggs
4½ oz (120g) caster sugar
3½ oz (85g) plain flour
1 oz (25g) chocolate powder
2 oz (50g) butter – melted and cooled

Filling: 2 egg yolks
   2½ oz (60g) caster sugar
   2½ fl oz (60 ml) water
   6 oz (175g) unsalted butter
   2 oz (50g) melted chocolate

8" (20 cm) cake tin

Place the eggs and sugar in a large bowl over a pan of simmering water.   Beat well until thick and frothy. Take off the heat and continue whisking.   Melt the butter and remove from heat. Sift the flour and chocolate powder and carefully fold most of it into the egg mixture.   Pour in the melted butter and quickly fold in the remaining flour.   Pour into an oiled 8 inch (20 cm) cake tin, lined with a round of paper and bake in pre-set oven at 190C/375F/Gas 5 for about 35 minutes until a skewer comes out clean.

Make the filling by dissolving the sugar in the water.   Boil till syrup becomes sticky (to a thread). Quickly pour it onto the beaten egg yolks, whisking until thick.   Cream butter, add the mousse carefully and then add the chocolate, which has been melted over hot water.   Split the cake and cover middle, top and sides with the cream.   Decorate or dust with sugar.

CHOCOLATE MOUSSE – QUICK*

14 oz (400g) plain dark chocolate
1 pint (570 ml) single cream
2 eggs
2 tbsp brandy or Cointreau
Decoration: 5 fl oz (150 ml) whipping cream

You need an electric blender to make this recipe

Break the chocolate into small pieces and put into a mixer.   Place the cream in a saucepan and bring to the boil.   Pour at once onto the broken chocolate pieces and process until smooth. Add the eggs and two tablespoons of liqueur.   Pour into individual ramekin dishes and leave in fridge.

Pipe on rosettes of whipped cream – preferably whipping cream as this is lighter than double cream.

CHOCOLATE NUT TARTLETS

Pastry: 7 oz (200g) margarine, 3 oz (75g) icing sugar,
           9 oz (250g) plain flour, 3 oz (75g) cornflour, 1 egg

Filling : 4 oz (110g) dark plain chocolate, 4 oz (110g) unsalted butter,
           4 oz (110g) caster sugar, 4 oz (110g) ground almonds, 1 egg

Icing: 4 oz (110g) white chocolate, 4 oz (110g) icing sugar

Mix margarine and icing sugar in mixer if possible and then add the flour, cornflour and egg. Mix quickly and leave in fridge for at least half an hour. Grease jam tart or miniature tins and line with the pastry. Grate the chocolate and then make the mixture by creaming the butter and adding the caster sugar, ground almonds, grated chocolate and egg. Fill the tarts – this is best done by piping it into the tins as there will be about 30 tartlets in all. Bake in a moderate oven for 20 to 30 mins. till the pastry browns and the filling rises.

Remove from oven and leave to cool while making the icing by melting the chocolate (dark chocolate could be used) with one or more tablespoons of water and stirring in sieved icing sugar. Smooth onto the centre of the tarts.

These can be served as a pudding and also with coffee. Some can be frozen for another day.

CHOCOLATE ROULADE

5 large eggs
8 oz (225g) caster sugar
6 oz (175g) Bournville or other plain chocolate

Filling:
  10 fl oz (300 ml) whipping cream
  2 tbsp Crème de Menthe or Amaretto liqueur

Swiss roll tin, baking parchment, icing sugar

Separate the eggs. Melt the chocolate in a shallow bowl over a saucepan of hot water. Add 3 tablespoons of hot water to the chocolate. Beat the yolks, add the caster sugar and beat well until very thick. Beat in the melted chocolate. Whip the whites and fold into the mixture with a metal spoon. Spread into a Swiss roll tin lined with parchment paper and bake for 20 minutes in a moderate oven (180C/350F/Gas 4) until the top is firm. Cool in the tin and leave in the fridge for several hours or overnight.

Sift some icing sugar onto a clean tea towel and turn the cake onto this. Whip the cream and add the liqueur. Remove the paper and spread the cake with the cream. Roll up carefully and slide onto a flat plate. Dust with icing sugar.

CHOCOLATE SAUCE

6 oz (175g) Bournville or other bitter chocolate
10 fl oz (300 ml) water
4 oz (110g) granulated sugar

Break up the chocolate and melt in the water over gentle heat. Add sugar, stir over low heat until dissolved. Simmer for at least l5 minutes. Leave to cool. This is a simple but excellent sauce.

CHOCOLATE SHORTCAKE

12 oz (335g) plain chocolate digestive biscuits
4 oz (110g) unsalted butter
3 tbsp chocolate powder
1 tbsp caster sugar
1 tbsp golden syrup

Crush biscuits and add to melted butter in a large pan with powder, sugar and syrup added.
Turn into an oblong tin, approx. 12 inches x 7 inches (30 cm x 18 cm) lined with foil. Mark into fingers and leave overnight in fridge, dusted with caster sugar. Cut out carefully and serve with cream.

This is an unusual quick pudding, which my daughter loves.

CHOCOLATE TART

Pastry: 11 oz (300g) plain flour
           6 oz (175g) unsalted butter
           3 oz (75g) caster sugar
           2 small eggs

Filling: 7 oz (200g) dark plain chocolate
           4 oz (110g) unsalted butter
           4 egg yolks
           1 egg white
           4 tbsp caster sugar

Make pastry by mixing flour and sugar together and adding butter in small pieces. Rub in, add the eggs and mix to a dough. Wrap in cling film and chill in fridge. Then bake blind in a 10" (25 cm) round flan dish by lining with foil and baking beans or rice and cooking for 10 minutes in a hot oven. Remove beans and foil and replace in oven for extra 5 minutes to cook the centre.

Meanwhile make the filling. Put broken chocolate in a bowl with butter over a pan of simmering water until just melted. Separate the eggs and cream the yolks and one egg white with the sugar in a large bowl, beating really well and then add the chocolate mixture and fold in gently. Pour into the pastry case, standing on a baking sheet and bake for 20 minutes at 180C/350F/Gas 4. Cool and dust with icing sugar. Serve with crème fraîche.

CHRISTMAS CAKE

8 oz (225g) sultanas*
6 oz (175g) crystallised fruit (pineapple, ginger etc)
4 oz (110g) glacé cherries, washed
4 oz (110g) candied peel
4 oz (110g) chopped walnuts
2 oz (50g) angelica, chopped
8 oz (225g) unsalted butter
8 oz (225g) caster sugar
Grated rind and juice of orange and lemon
4 eggs
8 oz (225g) plain flour
2 oz (50g) ground almonds

Soak overnight in 3 – 4 tbsp brandy or sherry

Prepare 8 inch (25 cm) cake tin by lining with double thickness of greaseproof paper and tying band of brown paper round outside one inch above edge.   Pre-heat oven to 180C/350F/Gas 4.   Mix all fruit together, chopping as necessary and quartering cherries.   Cream butter and sugar with rinds until fluffy.   Beat eggs till thick and add slowly to the creamed mixture.   Add a little sieved flour to fruits and stir rest into the creamed mixture and then add the fruit and nuts.   Add fruit juice and turn into tin, smoothing the top.   Bake for 1 hour and then put double sheet of greaseproof paper on top and turn down oven a little and cook for further 2 – 2 ¼ hours until skewer comes out clean.   Leave to cool in tin.

This is a light Christmas cake, but can still be made in advance.   Marzipan and ice later.

CHRISTMAS ICE CREAM

1 tbsp raisins and 1 tbsp sultanas soaked in 2 tbsp rum or other liqueur
1 tbsp finely chopped glacé cherries
1 tbsp finely chopped angelica
1 tbsp glacé pineapple, chopped
1 tbsp chopped peel
12 fl oz (350 ml) double cream
3 oz (75g) icing sugar, sifted
Tsp vanilla extract
4 egg whites

Mix all fruits together. Whip egg whites stiffly and then lightly whip the cream and fold in the egg whites and fruits and any liquid remaining from the rum.   Pour into a plastic container, ideally pudding shaped with a lid and put in freezer.   Stir when it starts to freeze and then return to freezer.

To serve – turn out on to a plate and return to freezer until needed.   Put a sprig of holly on the top. Ideal as a light alternative to Christmas Pudding.

CHRISTMAS LOG

3 large eggs
3 oz (50g) caster sugar
3 oz (75g) self-raising flour

Filling:
  5 fl oz (150 ml) double cream
  Small tin sweetened chestnut puree
  3 oz (75g) dark chocolate
Icing sugar

Whisk eggs and sugar for a long time until thick, light and fluffy.   Sieve the flour and fold into the creamed mixture with a metal spoon.   Pour into a Swiss roll tin lined with a piece of greaseproof or parchment paper.   Bake in a hot oven (220C/425F/Gas 7) for 10 to 15 minutes.   When set and coming away at edges turn out quickly onto sugared paper and roll up.

Melt chocolate over heat. Carefully unroll sponge and spread with a thin layer of chocolate. Whip the cream and stir in the chestnut puree. Spread on top of the chocolate and re-roll the sponge. Put any remaining cream on top of cake and make lines with a fork. Sieve over icing sugar.   If freezing, freeze first and then wrap in foil.

This is a quick cake to make and can be decorated with Father Christmas etc.

CHRISTMAS PUDDING*

12 oz (350g) mixed fruit and peel
2 oz (50g) glacé cherries, chopped
1 oz (25g) flaked almonds
2 oz (50g) suet
1½ oz (35g) white breadcrumbs
1½ oz (35g) plain flour
2½ oz (70g) brown sugar
2 oz (50g) cooking apple, grated
2 eggs, 3 tbsp ale, 3 tbsp brandy
Pinch of mixed spice and grated nutmeg
Juice of ½ lemon and ½ orange

Make in late October or early November and double the recipe for a 3 pint pudding.

Mix all the dry ingredients together, stir well and add the beaten eggs, fruit juice, ale and brandy. Stir very thoroughly and put into a well-buttered pudding basin (ideally 1½ pint size). Put a piece of buttered greaseproof paper over the pudding, then tie a piece of cloth securely over the top.   Or use a pudding basin with a lid.   Steam for 5 – 6 hours.   Leave in a cool place covered in foil.

On the day of your Christmas meal, steam for 3 hours. Turn out, pour over brandy, light it and put a sprig of holly on the top. Serve with brandy butter. Any left over can be reheated (sliced) in a hot oven with brandy butter spread on the top.

CHUTNEY

See also: Apple, Apricot, Mango and Orange

CHUTNEY – FRESH

Apple – crisp type
Tomato
Green Pepper
Half a cucumber
5 fl oz (150 ml) cider vinegar
Tbsp honey

Core and dice the apple, skin, de-seed and chop the tomato, pepper and cucumber into cubes. Mix the vinegar with the honey and pour over the vegetables. Serve with curries.

CHUTNEY - IRISH

3 lb (1.4 kg) marrow - peeled, quartered, seeded and diced
3 lb (1.4 kg) cooking apples, peeled, cored and chopped
8 oz (225g) onions, peeled and chopped, 1 clove garlic, crushed
4 lb (1.8 kg) granulated sugar
4 oz (110g) sultanas and 4 oz (110 g) raisins
4 oz (110g) dried apricots and 2 oz (50g) almonds, blanched and chopped
4 oz (110g) preserved ginger or 1 tbsp ground ginger
1 tbsp chillies, seeds removed and chopped or chilli powder
1 tbsp each of salt, ground cinnamon, ground cloves and nutmeg
30 fl oz (900 ml) malt vinegar and 5 tbsp whisky

Place all ingredients in large pan and bring to the boil stirring.   Reduce the heat and simmer for one and a half hours, stirring occasionally until chutney is thick and the consistency of jam.   Put into clean jars with screw tops. Try not to eat for a month or so!

COCKTAIL BISCUITS

2 oz (50g) rice crispies
6 oz (175g) plain flour
4 oz (110g) grated cheese
4 oz (110g) soft margarine or butter
1 small egg
1 tsp dried onion
1 tsp each of cayenne, mustard powder, celery and caraway seed

Mix all together, either by hand or in mixer.   Roll into strips.   Leave in fridge.   Cut into slices, put out in rounds on baking sheets and bake in a moderate oven for 15 minutes or a little longer.

Serve with drinks either by themselves, with pieces of cheese or with a dip.

COCKTAIL IDEAS

Blinis with crème fraîche and smoked salmon
Celery filled with cream cheese
Cheese biscuits
Cheese and pineapple pieces on cocktail sticks
Cheese puffs
Cocktail biscuits
Dips: Avocado
   Devil (Tartare sauce)
   Smoked mussel
Feta cheese tarts
Pizza pieces with anchovies
Prunes with bacon rolls
Spreads: Hummus
    Kipper pâté
    Liver pâté
    Smoked salmon pâté
    Tapenade
    Taramasalata
Vol-au-vent cases with savoury fillings

COD PORTUGUESE (2 – 4)

1 piece of cod per person
1 lb (450g) onions, sliced
Tin of chopped tomatoes or lb (450g) ripe tomatoes
Salt, pepper and parsley

Put pieces of cod in a buttered flat ovenproof dish. If using fresh tomatoes, skin and chop them. Fry onions and tomatoes in a little butter in a sauté pan.   Add seasoning and put on top of the fish. Cover with foil and cook in a moderate oven for about half an hour.   Alternatively, this could be made in a saucepan with the fish steamed on top of the tomatoes.

COLE SLAW

Small white cabbage, shredded
2 carrots, grated
Spring onions or red onion, chopped
1 or 2 stalks chopped celery
Sliced red and/or green pepper
Dressing:
 Salad cream mixed with little vinegar and milk

Put all the salad ingredients in a large bowl.   Dilute some bottled salad cream with a little milk and vinegar.   Shake to mix and pour over all the ingredients. Stir well and leave covered until needed. This is a quick salad, which keeps well.   Can be made with just cabbage and carrots.

COQ AU VIN (4 – 6)

Large roasting chicken
1 oz (25g) butter, tbsp oil
4 oz (110g) streaky bacon, diced
8 button onions
12 button mushrooms
Half bottle red wine
Clove garlic, crushed
Bay leaf, thyme, parsley
Salt, pepper,
2 tbsp flour and 2 tbsp butter (mixed together)

French loaf

Brown the chicken slowly in butter and oil.   Remove, add onions and bacon to the pan and brown while jointing the chicken.   Replace in pan.   Pour over the wine and flame.   Add garlic, herbs, mushrooms and seasoning.   Cook in oven slowly for about an hour.   Remove the chicken and vegetables and place in clean ovenproof dish. Thicken juices with kneaded butter and pour over the chicken. Fry some slices of French bread.

Reheat the chicken in the oven and serve surrounded by hot slices of the fried French bread with a salad or green vegetables.

CORNED BEEF HASH (2)*

Large potato or two medium potatoes
340g tin of Corned Beef
Tbsp olive oil, knob of butter
Onion
Clove of garlic
Mustard, Worcester sauce
Vegetable oil
Salt and pepper

This is worlds apart from the corned beef we used to have at school!

Par boil the potatoes for 3 – 5 mins and drain. Heat the butter and oil in a frying pan and cook the chopped onion and crushed garlic for about 10 mins until transparent.   Add the corned beef and cook until it starts to break down. Add a teaspoon of English mustard and a teaspoon of Worcester sauce. Remove from the pan and put into a bowl. Add vegetable oil to cover the base of the frying pan and sauté the potatoes, diced, over a hot heat browning well. Mix with the corned beef mixture and turn into a greased fireproof dish with plenty of seasoning.

Bake at 200C/400F/Gas 6 for 40 mins.

COTTAGE PIE (6)

2 lb (900g) minced beef
1 oz (25g) fat
1 large onion
8 oz (225g) mushrooms
1 green and/or red pepper
8 oz (225g) carrots
2 tins chopped tomatoes – 400g size
2 cloves garlic, crushed
Tbsp mustard and tbsp Worcester sauce
2 beef stock cubes
2 lb (900g) potatoes, mashed with butter and milk   .
   salt, pepper and nutmeg

Chop onions, mushrooms, carrots and pepper and sauté for about ten minutes in little dripping or fat as available in large frying pan or saucepan.   Add mince and garlic and continue frying, stirring well.   Add the tins of tomatoes, the stock cubes, Worcester sauce and mustard and simmer gently for about 30 minutes. Taste and add salt and pepper if necessary.   Meanwhile, cook the potatoes and drain and mash, adding the milk, butter and seasoning.

Put the mince mixture in an ovenproof pie or soufflé type dish and top with the mashed potatoes.

When needed cook for up to an hour in a moderate oven.

COURGETTE AND CHEESE SOUP

1 lb (450g) courgettes, trimmed and sliced
Large onion, skinned and chopped
¾ pint (450 ml) vegetable stock*
6 oz (175g) garlic and herb cheese (Philadelphia)
¼ pt (150 ml) single cream
Fresh herbs, such as parsley and/or coriander
Salt and ground black pepper

Marigold Swiss Vegetable Bouillon is very good

Put the sliced courgettes and chopped onion in a large saucepan with stock. Bring to the boil, lower the heat, cover the pan and simmer for 20 mins until the vegetables are soft.   Mix in the cheese and puree. A hand-held blender is very good for this as it saves washing up!   Chop the herbs finely, add the cream, salt and ground black pepper and reheat.

COURGETTE FRITTERS

6 small or 4 large courgettes
¼ pt (150 ml) milk
Seasoned flour
Vegetable or grapeseed oil*

This oil is very good for deep fat frying

Slice the courgettes and sprinkle with salt. Leave for about half an hour and then rinse and dry with a paper towel. Dip the slices first in the milk and then in the flour. Shake off the excess flour.

Put the oil about an inch deep in a frying pan or a sauté pan and get it really hot. Put in the courgette slices and remove once they are brown. Ideally serve at once.

COURGETTES WITH TOMATOES*

2 lb (900g) courgettes
Knob of butter and tbsp oil
1 lb tomatoes, skinned, seeded and diced
Small onion or 2 shallots
2 cloves chopped garlic
2 tbsp chopped parsley or basil
Salt and pepper
Breadcrumbs
Grated cheese

This is an excellent vegetable recipe as it can be prepared hours ahead ready to put into the oven

Slice the courgettes and, if time, sprinkle with salt. Leave to drain for about half an hour. Rinse and dry. Melt butter and oil in a large sauté pan and cook the courgettes for about 5 minutes until brown. Remove. Add the diced tomatoes, herbs, garlic and seasoning and cook till syrupy. Put courgettes and tomato mixture in a flat ovenproof serving dish. Cover with breadcrumbs and/or grated cheese and dot with butter.

Cook in a hot to moderate oven for half an hour or longer.

CRAB (4)

2 large crabs*
1½ oz (35g) butter and 1 oz (25g) flour
15 fl oz (450 ml) milk and 2 – 3 tbsp cream
2 hard boiled eggs, chopped
Tsp Dijon mustard and ½ tsp dry mustard
Tbsp Worcester sauce
Tbsp finely chopped parsley and tbsp finely chopped coriander
2 large shallots (chopped), salt, ground black pepper and cayenne

8 oz (225g) wild rice

Topping:
  Parmesan cheese

It is a good idea to freeze the shells as they could be used for prawn bisque or fish stock

Break off legs and claws from the crabs. Take meat from claws and shell, being sure to remove the dead man's fingers.   Make white sauce by melting the butter, adding the flour, cooking for one to two minutes and then stirring in the milk and cream until boiling.   Remove from heat and add all the other ingredients, except the rice.

Cook the wild rice in boiling water for about 30 minutes or the time given on the packet. Drain, pour over boiling water and fork into a buttered shallow ovenproof dish.   Pour over the crab mixture and top with grated Parmesan.   Reheat in hot oven for about 20 minutes.

CRAB FISH CAKES (4)

2 x 170g tins of crab
1½ lb Maris Piper (or similar) potatoes
Knob of butter, seasoning
2 tbsp capers
Finely grated zest of lemon

Flour, seasoning, egg and breadcrumbs

Cook and mash the potatoes, adding some butter and seasoning.   Drain the crab from the tins. Mix with the potatoes, add two tablespoons of well drained and chopped capers and the zest from a lemon.   Prepare three plates: one of well-seasoned flour, one of beaten egg and another of fresh breadcrumbs.   Form the mixture into eight rounds and coat in the flour, dip in the egg and finally cover in the breadcrumbs. Put on a baking sheet and leave in the fridge until needed.

Bake in a hot oven for about 20 mins till brown.   Serve with a salad. Any left over can be frozen and reheated at a later date.

CRANBERRY SAUCE

8 oz (225g) cranberries
Grated rind and juice of orange
5 fl oz (150 ml) water
Tbsp port
4 oz (110g) granulated sugar

Wash cranberries and place in a pan with all the ingredients. Bring slowly to the boil taking care to dissolve the sugar first and simmer until tender for about 10 minutes, bruising the cranberries with a wooden spoon. Put into a clear jar with a lid.

This will keep for about a week. If necessary it can be frozen.

Serve with roast turkey or roast pork.

CRÈME BRÛLÉE

1 pint (570 ml) double cream
4 egg yolks
5 tbsp caster sugar
1 split vanilla pod

*** This is a slightly tricky dish, but not difficult if made carefully**

Set oven at cool (150C/300F/Gas 2).   Put cream and vanilla pod in a basin over simmering water and bring up to the boil (scalding point). This will take about 20 minutes.   Mix yolks and tbsp of caster sugar with wooden spoon.   Remove pod and pour on cream, mix well and return to heat. Stir till it thickens over hot water – this could take 25 minutes.

Pour through sieve into ramekin dishes or one large white shallow ovenproof dish standing in a baking dish half filled with hot water. Put in oven for about 8 minutes until skin forms on the top. Remove at once and leave in fridge overnight.

The next day remove from fridge and cover the cream with the rest of the caster sugar. Preheat grill and put dish (or dishes) at least 4 inches away from the heat to brown. Watch carefully, turning as necessary. (Or use a professional blowtorch if you have one).   Cool.

 Serve with fruit and/or biscuits.

CRÈME CARAMEL (6)

Caramel:
    3 oz (75g) granulated sugar
    3 fl oz (75 ml) water

2 eggs and 2 yolks
1 pint (570 ml) milk
1 oz vanilla sugar* – or sugar and a few drops of vanilla extract

*** Vanilla sugar is easily made by keeping split vanilla pods in a jar of caster sugar.**

Take 6 ramekin dishes and put in a baking dish and heat in the oven.   Take a small saucepan and slowly melt the sugar in the water.   When melted boil until a rich brown colour.   Pour at once into the ramekin dishes, which have been removed from the oven.   Heat milk with the vanilla sugar. Beat the eggs and egg yolks and pour the heated milk onto them.   Mix well and put into a jug. Cool a little, sieve and then pour into the ramekin dishes on top of the caramel. Half fill the baking dish with hot water, cover dishes with greaseproof paper and put in a moderate oven for about 20 minutes until set.   Test with a knife, which should come out clean, but be careful not to overcook. Leave in the fridge.

Turn out on to individual dishes with a rim and serve with pouring cream.

This is a dish, which all men seem to love!

CRÊPES SUZETTE

Batter:
    6 oz (175g) plain flour
    1 egg and 1 egg yolk
    13 fl oz (375 ml) milk
    Tbsp brandy
    Tbsp melted butter

Sauce:
    4 oz (110g) unsalted butter
    6 oz (175g) caster sugar
    Grated rind and juice 2 oranges, 1 lemon
    2 tbsp Cointreau
    2 tbsp brandy

Make the batter, either in a mixer or in a large bowl, putting the flour round the edge and gradually beating in the milk, brandy and melted butter.   The consistency should be of thin cream, so do not add all the milk until sure it is necessary.   Make about 18 pancakes, keeping them as thin as possible.

Make the sauce by heating butter, sugar, rind and juices in a small saucepan.   Dissolve sugar gently and them simmer for 5 – 10 minutes. Add liqueurs. Fold pancakes into triangles. Put in a flat ovenproof dish.   Place in a very hot oven for a few minutes.   Reheat the sauce and pour over the pancakes and serve.

This dish can be frozen, but best if the pancakes and sauce are frozen separately.

CROUTONS

White loaf – 2 or 3 days old
Oil for frying
Clove of garlic

Cut the loaf into slices, stack them, remove the crusts and then cut the slices into small half inch cubes. Then heat a deep fat basket (if you have one) and cook in batches until light brown. Drain well on kitchen paper. Or, if preferred, put about 4 tbsp olive oil in a roasting tin, crush a clove of garlic into the oil and then toss the cubes of bread so that are coated with the oil. Heat in a moderate oven for about 10 minutes but watch them and turn them as necessary. Drain well. Reheat when needed.

It is a good idea to make a lot of croutons at once and keep small polythene bags of them in the freezer, so that they can be served with soups and salads.

CUMBERLAND SAUCE*

5 heaped tbsp redcurrant jelly
Tsp Dijon mustard
1 glass port or red wine
Juice of 1 orange and half a lemon
Shredded blanched strips of orange rind

Ham slices can be reheated in this sauce in an ovenproof dish covered with foil

Peel some of the orange with a potato peeler. Cut into strips and boil in small saucepan in some water. Heat redcurrant jelly slowly until melting, pour on the port, orange and lemon juice and whisk in the mustard. Finally, add the drained strips of orange rind. Serve cold with ham.

CURRIED EGGS

6 eggs, hard-boiled

Curry sauce:
    2 tbsp dripping or margarine
    2 tbsp flour, 2 tbsp curry powder, curry paste to taste
    12 fl oz (350 ml) stock
    2 medium onions, sliced
    2 tomatoes, skinned and chopped or small tin tomatoes
    1 large cooking apple, sliced, tbsp chutney, tbsp sultanas
    Worcester sauce, lemon juice, tsp sugar, salt and pepper

Cook onion and apple in fat in saucepan until brown. Add curry powder and flour, cook and then add stock (using stock cube if necessary) and bring to boil. Add other ingredients. Pour over halved hard-boiled eggs placed in a casserole dish and heat for an hour at least in a moderate to cool oven. Serve with plain rice – 2 oz per person – and side dishes (see under Curry)

CURRY – BEEF*

2 lbs (900g) beef – stewing or chuck steak
Small tin tomatoes
4 large Spanish onions
3 fresh green chillies or 6 dried chillies
Vegetable oil
4 bay leaves
2 tsp curry paste to taste
3 tsp cumin, 1½ tsp garlic powder
1 tsp chilli powder, 3 tsp turmeric
3 tsp coriander, 3 tsp garum masala

A Curry meal with beef, chicken, egg and vegetable curries with rice and side dishes is ideal when you have guests, one of whom is a vegetarian

Put a little oil in a large heavy bottomed saucepan and cook onions on a low heat. Mix the spices and add 10 fl oz (300 ml) water to make a paste. Add this to the onions with the tomatoes, bay leaves, chillies (from which all the seeds have been removed), chopped very finely and some curry paste. Cook gently while cutting up the beef into small pieces, removing fat and any gristle. Add the beef and cook slowly for 1½ hours on top of the stove or transfer to the oven. Top up with a little more water if necessary so that the meat is just covered. This can be made the day before and reheated.

Suggestions for side dishes:

　　Banana slices, dipped in lemon juice
　　Chutneys
　　Coconut – grated
　　Pineapple – cubed
　　Peanuts
　　Poppodums – cooked in hot fat
　　Tzatziki

See also:
　　Marrow curry
　　Thai chicken curry
　　Turkey in a curry sauce (cold)
　　Vegetable curry

DILL SAUCE

3 tbsp Dijon mustard
2 tsp caster sugar
3 tbsp cider vinegar
1 tsp salt
5 fl oz (150 ml) oil – sunflower or groundnut
4 tbsp fresh dill, finely chopped

Stir mustard, sugar, vinegar and salt together and then slowly whisk in the oil.
Finally add the chopped dill.

Can be kept in the fridge in a jar. It is delicious with gravadlax.

DROP SCONES (makes about 12)

4 oz (110g) self-raising flour
2 tsp baking powder
Tbsp caster sugar
1 egg
Tsp golden syrup
7 tbsp milk
Vegetable oil

Sift the flour and baking powder into a bowl. Add the sugar and make a well. Mix the golden syrup, egg and milk and gradually add this to the powder mixture to make a batter. Whisk and add a little more milk if necessary to make a dropping consistency. Leave.

Heat a griddle pan or a heavy frying pan with a little oil for about five minutes. Drop the mixture in spoonfuls. Leave for a few minutes until set, then turn over to cook the other side pressing them down well. Remove when brown.

Eat as soon as possible – delicious with butter and honey. Any left over can be frozen and reheated.

DUCK BREASTS IN CREAM SAUCE (4)

3 large duck breasts
1 onion or shallot
5 fl oz (150 ml) white wine
10 fl oz (300 ml) double cream
5 fl oz (150 ml) chicken stock
2 tbsp green peppercorns
Salt

Place breasts in roasting pan and prick all over. Cook in hot oven (200C/400F/Gas 6) for about 20 minutes. Leave to cool, having strained off fat into the frying pan. Remove skins, cut into small pieces and fry in the fat until crisp. Place on Pyrex or tin plate and leave ready to reheat.

Carve the duck into slices and place in a flat ovenproof dish. Cover with foil. Make sauce by chopping the onion or shallot and simmering in the wine for about 5 minutes. Add stock and peppercorns and cream. Add little salt and taste. Leave.

Before the meal, reheat meat in moderate oven and put fat skins at top of oven. Just before serving, reheat sauce, pour over the duck and top with the fat pieces. Serve with new potatoes and a salad or a green vegetable.

DUMPLINGS

4 oz (110g) self-raising flour or
    plain flour with tsp baking powder
2 oz (50g) beef suet
Tsp salt
Handful of parsley, if available

Mix all ingredients in a bowl with finely chopped parsley if using. Add little water very slowly, mixing as you go to a stiff firm paste, which should be firm and not wet. Roll into balls (this amount can make as many as ten or eleven) and leave on a flat plate in the fridge until needed.

Place on top of a casserole, like beef stew, baste with the gravy and cook with the lid off for about 45 minutes.

EGG POTS (6)

6 hard-boiled eggs, chopped
8 oz (225g) prawns
¼ small jar Dijon mustard
10 fl oz (300 ml) double cream
Handful of parsley, chopped
6 oz (175g) grated cheese, mixture of Gruyere and Parmesan

Take 6 small ovenproof pots or ramekin dishes.   Mix the cream and mustard, add the chopped eggs, prawns and parsley and divide into the dishes.   Top with the cheese and just before serving put under hot grill until bubbling.

EGGS – BAKED

1 egg per person
Tins of: baked beans, asparagus, sweet corn or artichoke hearts
Choice of: mushrooms, tomatoes, bacon or sliced cooked potatoes
Salt and pepper

Topping: Little cream, butter or grated cheese

Take a flat ovenproof dish.   Put a layer of baked beans etc. in the bottom. Add any other suitable ingredients, putting bacon and sliced cooked potatoes (if you have them) round the edges.   Make indentations for the eggs and place them carefully in the dish.   Add seasoning and a little cream, butter and/or grated cheese.   Place in a moderate oven and cook until the eggs are set – about 20 minutes. Serve at once with bread and butter.   This is an easy instant dish.

EGGS FLORENTINE (2)

9 oz (250g) fresh spinach, cooked and chopped
    or 5 oz (125g) frozen spinach
3 tomatoes, peeled and sliced
3 hard-boiled eggs, sliced
Cheese sauce made with large knob of butter,
    heaped tbsp flour, cup of milk and handful of grated cheese
    salt, pepper, little mustard powder and grated nutmeg

Topping: Parmesan cheese and breadcrumbs

Set oven to 200C/440F/Gas 6. Put spinach on the base of an oven dish and cover with slices of tomato and hard-boiled eggs.   Make the cheese sauce by melting the butter, stirring in the flour, cooking for a minute or two and then pouring on the milk.   Bring slowly to the boil and then add the grated cheese and seasonings.   Pour over the dish and finally top with some breadcrumbs, mixed with one or two tablespoons of Parmesan cheese, and a little butter.   Cook for at least 30 minutes. This is a good all-in-one dish.

EGGS IN ASPIC

1 poached egg per person, trimmed
Strips of smoked or Parma ham
Gherkin slices or similar to decorate
Tarragon or basil leaves
Tin of consommé
Half pkt gelatine diluted with tbsp sherry

One ramekin dish per person

Poach the eggs, cool, trim and place carefully in ramekin dishes, on top of strips of ham.
Put little sherry and gelatine in small dish and melt over hot water.   At the same time melt the
consommé.   Cool and stir in the gelatine. Pour on top of eggs slowly and carefully. Leave
a little behind and when the gelatine starts to set, decorate and finally add the remainder of the
liquid.

Leave in fridge, but remove a little while before serving.

Serve with garlic bread or rolls.

EGGS WITH CAVIAR

1 egg per person, hard-boiled
Slices pumpernickel bread
Small jar of Danish caviar (lumpfish)
Mayonnaise
Watercress or lambs lettuce
Lemon quarters

On each plate put a slice of the pumpernickel surrounded by some lettuce or watercress.
Cut the hard-boiled eggs (which should have been peeled and kept in a bowl of cold water) in half
long ways and place yolk side up on the bread.   Pipe or put on some mayonnaise and top with
spoonfuls of the caviar. Serve with the lemon quarters.

An easy starter, which looks attractive.

FENNEL

Fennel can be added to salad as long as it is cut into small pieces and only a small amount used as it has a very strong flavour. It can also be braised. Take 3 bulbs, remove outer skin, core and leaves and steam until tender for about 5 – 10 minutes. Cool. Slice and put in a shallow ovenproof dish with butter. Cook in a moderate oven for about half an hour.

FETA CHEESE TARTS

Pastry: 6 oz (175g) plain flour, pinch salt
            4 oz (110g) butter
            Egg white
Filling: 3 fl oz (75 ml) double cream
            3 egg yolks, salt
            Large pinch cayenne pepper
            Chopped coriander or parsley
            4 oz (110g) feta cheese
            7 sun-dried tomatoes

Make pastry by sifting flour and salt into a bowl. Melt butter and pour onto flour, mixing with a wooden spoon. Add egg white and stir until the dough is smooth. Leave to cool for up to five minutes. Divide into l2 pieces and press into jam tart tins so that they go over the edge.

Leave in fridge while preparing the filling. Beat cream and egg yolks until starting to thicken, then whisk in flavouring, the crumbled feta cheese and the chopped herbs. Slice the tomatoes and add with some seasoning. Spoon into the tins and cook in a moderate to hot oven for 30 minutes until brown. Good for picnics or supper, as well as with drinks.

FETTUCINE WITH GOATS` CHEESE (4)

8 oz (225g) fettucine or other pasta
1 lb (450g) cherry tomatoes
2 tbsp olive oil, ground pepper and salt
4 oz (100g) soft goats` cheese
Pesto:
     2 oz (50g) basil leaves
     2 oz (50g) pine nuts
     2 cloves garlic, crushed
     2 oz (50g) Parmesan, grated
     5 fl oz (150 ml) extra-virgin olive oil

Put the tomatoes in a roasting tin, drizzle with 2 tbsp olive oil and season well. Cook in a hot oven till soft and a bit charred for about 40 mins. Put basil, nuts, garlic and half of the Parmesan into a mixer and blend adding the olive oil gradually. Finally stir in the rest of the Parmesan. Break up the goat`s cheese and add to the pesto.  Cook the pasta in boiling salted water for about ten mins.  Drain, pour over hot water and then mix with the pesto and goats` cheese and the tomatoes. Serve at once or put in a fireproof dish to be reheated. Serve with a salad. This dish freezes well.

FIGS WITH WINE

10 black figs
4 fl oz (110 ml) red wine
4 oz (110g) granulated sugar
2 fl oz (50 ml) water
Brandy or Cointreau

Make a syrup of wine and sugar and a little water.   Bring slowly to the boil, being careful to melt the sugar first and continue boiling until thickened.   Put in the figs, which you have peeled, and poach for 5 minutes, turning over once or twice in the syrup. Cool.   Remove the figs and place in an attractive shallow bowl.   Reduce the liquid by boiling again for a few minutes and add some brandy or other liqueur. Cool and then pour over figs. Serve chilled with cream.

FISH PIE (6)

1½ lb (675g) mixture of smoked haddock and cod
½ lb (225g) prawns
3 eggs
12 oz (335g) tomatoes
1½ lb (625g) spinach or 1 lb (450g) frozen spinach
Salt and pepper
3 oz (75g) butter
3 oz (75g) flour
16 fl oz (475 ml) milk

Topping: 2 lb potatoes, such as Maris Piper or King Edwards
          Butter, milk and seasoning

Large pie dish

Cook the fish in a large sauté pan in the milk for about ten minutes. Drain and keep the milk for the white sauce. Hard boil the eggs, cool, peel and slice. Skin the tomatoes by putting them for a minute in boiling water and then cooling in cold water. Slice. Cook the spinach (if fresh) and drain well. Make a white sauce with the milk, adding a little more milk if too thick and flake the drained fish into it together with the prawns.

Butter a large pie dish and add the drained spinach and top with the fish mixture. Then add the sliced eggs and tomatoes. Finally cook the potatoes and mash them well, adding butter, milk and seasoning. Spread over the top of the pie forking it and pressing down the sides.   Dot with butter.

Reheat in a hot – moderate oven for at least half an hour until really hot and the potatoes are brown.

Serve as it is or with a green salad.

FISH PIE – EASY (4)

4 frozen cod steaks (or other white fish)
1½ oz (35g) butter, 1½ oz (35g) flour
10 fl oz (300 ml) or more milk
Tbsp tomato ketchup, tbsp Worcester sauce
Topping: Croutons, mashed potatoes or cheese and breadcrumbs

Cover the fish with the milk.   Cook and then leave to cool.   Make roux with the butter and flour and pour on the strained milk. Bring to the boil stirring well so that there are no lumps. Add heaped tablespoon each of tomato ketchup and Worcester sauce. Meanwhile flake the fish and place in a small soufflé dish. Pour over the sauce and then top with croutons.   Croutons can either be made with cubes of bread fried in oil or baked in the oven with a little garlic crushed into the oil. Watch carefully and turn.   Freeze any surplus.   Alternatively, put mashed potatoes or a mixture of cheese and breadcrumbs on the top of the fish mixture. Put the dish in a hot oven for 20 – 30 mins.

FLAPJACKS

8 oz (225g) butter or margarine or a mixture
8 oz (225g) Demerara sugar, pinch salt
8 oz (225g) Quaker or Scotts oats
1 oz (25g) desiccated coconut

Place butter and sugar in saucepan and melt gently.   Add the rest of the ingredients and stir well. Press into a buttered Swiss roll type tin.   Bake in a cool to moderate oven until beginning to brown. This will take about 30 minutes.   Remove from oven, leave to cool and then mark into pieces. Cut and remove from tin when completely cold.   Keep in an airtight tin.

FONDUE – BEEF

Rump Steak – 6 oz (175g) per person cut into cubes
Oil – vegetable or corn for frying
Individual salads, celery, olives etc.

SAUCES:

CURRY:	Mix tbsp whipped cream with 3 tbsp mayonnaise, tsp curry powder, tbsp chutney
HORSERADISH:	Mix 5 tbsp sour cream with 2 – 3 tbsp grated horseradish or creamed horseradish
MUSTARD:	Mix 4 tbsp sour cream with 3 – 4 tbsp mayonnaise and 2 – 3 tsp Dijon mustard

Take out fondue equipment and place on hot mat on table. Take the bowl and fill with oil half full and add a small raw potato, which keeps down the smell.   Heat the fat to 180C on stove and place on table when needed.   Be sure everyone knows to use an ordinary fork as well as the fondue fork. Serve with a selection of sauces, bread and salads.

FONDUE – CHEESE*

SWISS:

1 1b (450g) grated cheese:
    40% Gruyere, 40% Emmental, 20% Appenzell
8 fl oz (225 ml) white wine
3 tbsp kirsch
Pepper, grated nutmeg and paprika
Lemon juice, tsp cornflour
French bread

Traditionally this is always made by the man of the house!

Have the fondue set ready and topped up with methylated spirits and placed on a hot mat on the table. Rub the bowl with garlic. Put in the cheese with teaspoon of cornflour, lemon juice, black pepper and nutmeg. Put on the kitchen stove and pour over the wine and stir until boiling. Add kirsch and transfer to the fondue set. Serve with French bread cut into large cubes.

ENGLISH:

For a less expensive English version, make in the same way as above but use the following:

Knob of butter
10 fl oz (300 ml) cider
1 tbsp cornflour
12 oz (335g) Cheddar cheese, grated
2 tbsp kirsch or Calvados (optional)
Black pepper, clove garlic, crushed
French bread

FRANKFURTER CASSEROLE (4)

8 or more frankfurters, sliced
3 slices bacon
Large tin baked beans
Large onion, sliced
Knob of butter
Small tin tomatoes or 3 tomatoes skinned and sliced
Tsp curry powder, salt and pepper
Salt and pepper

Fry sliced onion in butter. Add the bacon, cut into strips and fry for one minute. Stir in the curry powder and fry for another minute. Add the sliced frankfurters, the baked beans, seasoning and tomatoes. Put into an ovenproof dish and bake in a moderate oven for at least half an hour. Serve with baked potatoes.

FRENCH APPLE FLAN

Pastry: 8 oz (225g) plain flour
                    4 oz (110g) butter
                    4 oz (110g) caster sugar (vanilla if possible)
                    2 egg yolks
Apple puree: 1 lb (450g) cooking apples, peeled and cored
                    1 tbsp water
                    3 oz (75g) sugar
                    2 oz (50g) butter
                    2 – 3 tbsp Calvados
Filling: 1 lb (450g) dessert apples
                    Juice of 2 lemons
Glaze: 2 tbsp apricot jam
                    2 tbsp water

Prepare the pastry in mixer or by hand, by mixing cut up butter into the flour and sugar until it resembles breadcrumbs. Then add the two egg yolks to make a dry paste and leave to chill in fridge for about an hour. Meanwhile make the puree by chopping the apples, putting them on a low heat with the water. Cook slowly, covered with a buttered paper and a lid till fluffy. Mash into a puree and add sugar and then butter little by little stirring and finally add 2 – 3 tablespoons of Calvados.

Line a large 10" – 11" (25 cm – 23 cm) flan dish with the pastry, bake blind by lining the pastry with foil and some baking beans or rice and cooking for about 5 minutes in a moderate oven. Fill flan with the puree, then top with the dessert apples, sliced and tossed in lemon juice. Return to the oven for about 30 minutes till brown. Heat jam in saucepan with water and remains of the lemon juice. Remove the flan from the oven and carefully sieve over the apricot jam glaze.

Serve the flan warm or cold with cream.

FRENCH DRESSING

Make a large quantity in a bottle as follows:

1/3rd white wine vinegar
2/3rd oil, mixture of groundnut or sunflower and olive
Tsp salt
Tsp sugar
Tsp Dijon mustard
Clove of garlic, crushed
Freshly ground black pepper

Pour all ingredients into a bottle, with a funnel if necessary. Shake well and keep in the fridge. This can of course be adapted as liked and ingredients available. Lemon juice can be used instead of the vinegar and herbs can be added. But the above recipe keeps well.

FRUIT CAKE – BOILED

1½ lb (675g) dried fruit mixture (sultanas, raisins, currants, mixed peel)
8 oz (225g) sugar – brown or mixture brown and caster
8 oz (225g) butter or margarine
1 lb (450g) self-raising flour
10 fl oz (300 ml) water
3 large or 4 small eggs
Grated rind of orange and/or lemon

9" (23 cm) round cake tin or 2 x 6" (15 cm) cake tins, lined with greaseproof paper.

Put fruit, water, butter and sugar in a large saucepan. Stir and bring to the boil.   Simmer for 20 minutes stirring occasionally. Cool for about 30 minutes. Then add the beaten eggs, sieved flour and rind. Mix well and pour into tin or tins.

Bake in moderate oven (150C/300F/Gas 2) for 2½ to 3 hours for a large cake or 1½ to 2 hours for small cakes.   Test if done with a skewer, which should come out clean.   Remove and leave to cool in tin before turning out.   Wrap in foil and keep in an airtight tin.

This is a quick easy cake to make which keeps very well.

FRUIT SALAD

Melon or pineapple
2 oranges or tangerines and a grapefruit
2 peaches or nectarines
1 or 2 pears
1 or 2 apples
1 or 2 bananas
2 kiwi fruit and 2 passion fruit
Black and/or white grapes
Strawberries or raspberries
Lemon juice
2 – 3 tbsp liqueur

A fruit salad is delicious if it is totally fresh and as long as enough juicy fruit is used there is no need to make a syrup.   The fruit should be cut into different shapes and slices and bananas and and apples should be dipped in lemon juice to avoid them going brown.   A little brandy or other liqueur adds to the flavour. It should be put in an attractive glass bowl, covered in cling film and kept in the fridge until needed.

In winter nuts and dates can be added and if fresh fruit is not available a berry fruit salad can be made from frozen raspberries, redcurrants, blackcurrants and blackberries and possibly blueberries.   Do not use frozen strawberries, which are horrible!

GAMMON STEAK

1 Gammon steak per person
Dried mustard
Demerara sugar
Cloves

Trim the gammon steaks, taking off any rind etc. and make a few cuts into the edges.   Lay them flat in a shallow ovenproof dish.   Sprinkle each steak with dried mustard and about 2 teaspoons of Demerara sugar and 3 – 4 cloves.

Heat in moderate oven for 20 minutes.   Serve with mashed potatoes and a green vegetable.

GARLIC AND HERB LOAF

1 French loaf
4 oz (110g) salted butter
Handful of herbs, chopped
2 – 3 cloves of garlic, crushed
Tbsp lemon juice
Black pepper

Warm the butter and mix with the chopped herbs and crushed garlic.   Add the lemon juice and some ground black pepper.   Cut the loaf into slices, spread with the butter mixture. Wrap the loaf in foil and put into a hot oven on a baking sheet, with an edge, and cook for 10 minutes.   Then turn the oven down to moderate, open out the foil and leave for 8 minutes or longer.

GAZPACHO (4)

2¼ lb (1 kg) very ripe tomatoes
Salt and pepper
Selection of vegetables: cucumber, radishes, red pepper
                            spring onions, cherry tomatoes
                            avocado and/or apple
Selection of herbs: chopped basil, coriander and/or chervil

Put the tomatoes in a blender with plenty of seasoning and turn on briefly. Put a sieve, lined with muslin, over a large bowl and put in the tomato mixture. Leave overnight or longer in the fridge. Press the tomatoes down well and use the drained liquid for the soup.

Cut up the vegetables as small as possible in different shapes. If using cherry tomatoes, cut them in half. Put into a little of the tomato water to stop browning. Chop the herbs finely. Leave everything in the fridge.

To serve divide the vegetables into 4 bowls. Divide the tomato water between each bowl.

GOAT'S CHEESE WITH FIGS (4)

Packet of mixed leaves with some red colour
3 ripe figs
8 pieces of goat's cheese
8 slices of Parma ham
4 tbsp French dressing

Cut the figs into quarters and the goat's cheese into 8 pieces. Toss the salad with the dressing and put onto four small plates for a first course. Add 3 pieces of fig, 2 pieces of the cheese and two slices of the Parma ham to each plate. Serve with rolls and/or breads.

GOOSEBERRY FOOL (4)

1 lb (450g) fresh gooseberries
Tbsp water
3 tbsp brown sugar
5 fl oz (150 ml) double cream

Top and tail the gooseberries with scissors and put in a saucepan with sugar and water, stirring occasionally until fruit is soft. If you have any elderflower berries, add these to the gooseberries, but remove them at the end of the cooking time. They have a delicious flavour. Remove the gooseberries from the heat and leave to cool a little. If there is a lot of juice remove some and then push the cooked gooseberries through a sieve to make a puree. Whip the cream and mix with the puree. Taste and add more sugar if necessary. Put into 4 glass bowls and leave in fridge.

Serve with homemade Viennese biscuits or packet wafers.

GOUGERE (3 – 4)

4 oz (110g) butter
5 fl oz (150 ml) each water and milk
Tsp salt
5 oz (150g) plain white flour (sifted)
4 small or 3 large eggs
Black pepper
3 oz (75g) finely grated Gruyere and Parmesan cheese mixed

Put butter, milk, water and teaspoon of salt in a saucepan. Bring to the boil and boil for half a minute stirring with a wooden spoon. Remove from the heat and tip in all the flour at once. Beat until smooth and return to heat continuing to beat for another minute. Remove and put in a bowl. Leave to cool a little and then beat eggs in one at a time till the mixture is shiny. Add the grated cheese and some ground pepper. Put in a large ovenproof dish leaving space in the centre for a filling such as ham and mushroom or prawn and tomato (See pages 138 and 139). Dust with grated cheese and leave until ready to bake. Heat oven to 200C/400F/Gas 6 and cook for about 40 minutes until well risen and firm. Eat at once with a green salad.

GOULASH (6)

2 lb (900g) cubed chuck steak
Tbsp flour
Tsp paprika
3 tbsp oil
2 cloves garlic, crushed
2 large onions, sliced
2 large carrots, sliced
1 red pepper, chopped
Tin of tomatoes – 400g size
10 fl oz (300 ml) liquid – stock and/or red wine
Bay leaf, thyme, parsley
Salt and pepper

Coat steak cubes in a mixture of flour and paprika. Brown in hot oil. Remove and place in a casserole dish. Then fry crushed garlic, sliced onions, carrots and chopped pepper. Sauté for 5 minutes, then add tomatoes, stock, herbs and salt and pepper. Bring to the boil and then pour over the meat in the casserole. Cover and cook in a moderate oven for about 2 hours.

Serve with rice, noodles or baked potatoes.

GRAVADLAX

Small salmon*
4 tbsp brandy
2 tbsp coarse sea salt
Tbsp white sugar
2 tsp ground white pepper
2 oz (50g) fresh dill

Extra wide foil

Ask the fishmonger to halve and fillet the salmon

Put one fillet skin side down on a large piece of foil in a dish or tray with an edge. Remove any bones with a pair of tweezers or fingers. Mix salt, sugar and pepper together and sprinkle half of this mixture and half of the brandy over the fish. Cover with dill and the remainder of the ingredients. Place other half of fish on top with skin side up. Cover whole as tightly as possible with the foil and put about 4 lb weight or weights on top. Put in fridge and turn once or twice a day for 2 – 3 days, basting with any leaking juices.

Remove foil, wipe off mixture and slice. Any leftovers could be frozen if necessary. Serve with dill sauce (see page 61) and brown bread and butter or rolls.

GREEK SALAD

1 lb (450g) ripe tomatoes
1 cucumber
1 small green pepper
1 white or red salad onion
Black olives
Feta cheese cubes
Olive oil, lemon juice
Salt and pepper
Basil and/or other herbs

Chop the tomatoes roughly and add pieces of cubed cucumber and top with diced onion.   Add the black olives and pieces of feta cheese.   Top with little lemon juice, olive oil, salt, pepper and herbs, such as basil, if available.

One gets tired of this salad in Greece, but it is good as a change in England!

GUINEA FOWL (6)

2 guinea fowl
2 oz (50g) butter
2 oz (50g) flour
2 onions, peeled and coarsely chopped
3 stalks of celery, chopped
1 large cooking apple, peeled and chopped
5 fl oz (150 ml) dry cider
2 tbsp Calvados
Chicken or game stock – 10 fl oz (300 ml) or more
6 tbsp double cream or crème fraîche
Salt and pepper

Cut each fowl into 8.   Dust with the flour and brown in the butter over high heat in flameproof casserole.   Lower heat and add onions, celery and apple.   Cook for 5 minutes, then remove from the heat and stir in any remaining flour.   Cook for a further 3 minutes.   Slowly add the cider, Calvados and half a pint of stock.   Gradually bring to the boil and simmer gently for about 10 minutes.   Season and, if necessary, add more stock so as to cover the fowl.   Put in a moderate oven for 45 minutes covered.

Leave to cool a little and then remove some of the bones from the guinea fowl and place in a flat ovenproof dish.   Put the casserole dish on the top of the stove and boil the sauce hard to reduce. Then add the cream and seasoning and pour over the fowl.   Cover with foil and reheat when needed.

Good with mashed potato and a green vegetable or salad.

HADDOCK SUPREME (2 – 3)

1 lb (450g) haddock fillet
1 oz (25g) butter
4 oz (110g) carrots
2 oz (50g) turnips
2 tomatoes, stick celery
1 slice onion, bay leaf, seasoning
Sauce: 1 oz (25g) butter, 1 oz (25g) flour
       7 fl oz (200 ml) milk

Wash and dice all vegetables, except tomatoes. Melt knob of butter in oven dish, which goes on top of stove. Add vegetables and seasoning and cook gently 3 – 4 minutes. Add tomatoes, skinned and sliced. Place in low to moderate oven. After 30 minutes, add skinned fish, cut into 4 pieces and dot with little butter. Lay bay leaf on top. Cook for 20 minutes.   Strain off juice, remove bay leaf and make a sauce by melting the butter, adding the flour, cooking for a minute and then adding the strained juice and the milk. Bring to the boil, stirring and coat the fish and vegetables and serve.

HALIBUT WITH BEANS (4)

1½ lb (675g) halibut, cut into squares*
1½ lb (675g) French or runner beans*
Tin of condensed tomato soup

Any white frozen fish and frozen beans could be used for this very easy recipe.

Cook beans for about 5 minutes. Place fish in a casserole dish with the beans. Place soup in saucepan with 3 tablespoons water and bring to the boil, stirring and pour on to the fish. Cover and cook for 30 minutes. Serve with a baked potato.

HALIBUT WITH VEGETABLES (3)

1 lb (450g) halibut
1 clove garlic, crushed and small onion, chopped
1 green pepper, sliced thinly
1 stick celery, chopped
Small tin tomatoes or 4 tomatoes, skinned and sliced
8 oz (225g) sliced mushrooms
5 fl oz (150 ml) white wine
2 tbsp lemon juice, 3 tbsp soy sauce
2 tbsp oil, salt and pepper

Heat the oil and cook the onion, pepper, garlic and celery until soft.   Add the tomatoes, lemon juice, soy sauce and wine.   Simmer for 5 minutes and then add the mushrooms.   Leave to cool. Season to taste.   Place halibut in a flat ovenproof dish.   Pour over the vegetables and sauce. Bake in hot oven for 15 – 20 minutes.

HAM

See also: Gammon Steaks
            Leeks and ham
            Pancakes with ham
            Rice with Ham
            Spaghetti with ham
            Vol-au-Vent

HAM – BAKED

Gammon joint
3 tbsp brown sugar

Wide foil

Soak joint of gammon in water for up to an hour or rinse if time is short.   Drain.   Wrap tightly in two large pieces of foil.   Put in large baking tin with a cup of water.

Bake in a hot oven (200C/400F/Gas 6) for half an hour for each pound.   Turn parcel over at half time.   Remove foil and skin.   Save a little of the juice and mix to a paste with brown sugar, make criss-cross cuts in the fat (score) and smear on the sugar.   Return to oven to brown.

Carve and serve as a joint with Cumberland sauce (see page 57), roast vegetables and a green vegetable.

HAM SALAD WITH CHEESE

Half iceberg lettuce, sliced
2 tomatoes, sliced
2 heads of chicory, sliced
2 tbsp fresh parsley, chopped
1 green apple, chopped
Handful of croutons – see page 57
8 oz (225g) cooked ham, sliced and chopped
6 oz (175g) Edam or Emmental cheese, cubed
French dressing

Prepare all the salad ingredients, leaving skin on the apple.   Put in a large bowl and then add the pieces of ham, the cubed cheese and some croutons.   Pour over French dressing made by mixing a tablespoon of wine vinegar with teaspoon sugar, small clove of garlic, crushed, a tablespoon of whole grain mustard, a pinch of salt and 3 tablespoons of olive oil.   Stir all together very well and serve.

An excellent one-dish meal.

HAM WITH FIGS (6)

10 small slices of good ham
4 ripe figs
2 packets of rocket
Small packet of pistachio nuts

Dressing: 2 tbsp extra-virgin olive oil
           Tbsp sesame, walnut or hazelnut oil
           Tbsp red wine vinegar
           Tbsp cold water
           Ground pepper and salt

Slice the ham into narrow strips and quarter the figs. Shell the nuts and make the dressing.
Toss the rocket with half the dressing and put on 6 individual plates for a first course. Add the ham, figs and nuts and pour over the rest of the dressing. Serve with rolls.

HAM WITH JUNIPER BERRIES (6 – 8)

2 thick slices of ham per person
4 shallots
6 juniper berries
6 tbsp wine vinegar
1½ oz (35g) butter
1½ oz (35g) flour
10 fl oz (300 ml) chicken stock
10 fl oz (300 ml) white wine
5 fl oz (150 ml) double cream

Crush berries, chop shallots very finely and put in a small saucepan with the vinegar.   Boil until vinegar has almost boiled away. In another saucepan, make roux by melting the butter, adding the flour, cooking a little and then stirring in the chicken stock, wine and the vinegar mixture. Stir and bring to the boil, then simmer gently, stirring occasionally, for about 20 minutes.   Then sieve, add the cream and season to taste.

Put the ham slices in a flat casserole dish. Pour over the sauce and cover with a lid. Reheat in a low to moderate oven for at least 30 minutes.

This is a good recipe for a dinner party, especially if served with vegetable pie, when it can all be made in advance

HAM WITH REDCURRANT SAUCE

Slices of cooked ham

Red-currant jelly, some port or red wine
             or
Cumberland sauce

This is a simple quick version of the previous recipe – useful for using up a ham joint.

Take some thick slices of cooked ham – two per person – and layer them in a shallow ovenproof dish. Melt some redcurrant jelly and mix with some port or red wine, making enough to just cover the slices. Or alternatively use Cumberland sauce. Cover the dish with a piece of foil. Cook in a moderate oven for about 30 minutes

Serve with a baked potato. A few sliced peaches could be added to the ham.

HAZELNUT MERINGUE GATEAU

4 large egg whites
9 oz (250g) vanilla caster sugar*
½ tsp white wine vinegar
4 oz (110g) ground hazelnuts
10 fl oz (300 ml) double cream
Icing sugar

2 x 8" (20 cm) sandwich tins, lined, oiled and floured

This is easily made by keeping some vanilla pods in a jar of caster sugar

Whip egg whites until stiff and add sugar, a tablespoon at a time, until half is mixed in and mixture is shiny and very stiff.   Mix rest of the sugar with the hazelnuts and fold into egg whites together with half a teaspoon of vinegar. Put into the prepared tins. Bake in moderate oven (350F/160C/Gas 4) for 40 minutes being careful they do not burn.   Remove from oven and leave to cool before turning out.

About 3 hours before serving fill with whipped cream and decorate top with cream rosettes and hazelnuts. Can be served with fresh fruit, like raspberries, or with chocolate sauce, or together with apricot mousse.

The meringue rounds can be kept in an airtight tin for about a week if necessary.

HEDGEHOG PUDDING

Meringue: 8 oz (225g) caster sugar
                 4 egg whites

Caramel: 4 heaped tbsp caster sugar
                 2 tbsp water

Topping: Whipped cream
                 Almonds – toasted

Put 4 tablespoons caster sugar and 2 tablespoons water in small saucepan, melt sugar slowly and then turn up heat to high to make caramel. Watch carefully and when brown pour into a pudding bowl – about 2 pint size – which has been warmed. Leave to cool.

Meanwhile beat the egg whites until very stiff, beating in half the sugar. Fold in the rest of the sugar and put on top of the caramel. Put into a saucepan of 2 inches of boiling water, put on the lid firmly and after a minute turn off heat and leave on the stove until the next day.

Turn the pudding onto a plate with a rim, pour over the caramel (reheat if necessary). Top with whipped cream and decorate with toasted almonds.

I have only had this at my Aunt`s house, but it apparently originated from the Rothschilds.

HOLLANDAISE SAUCE*

8 oz (225g) unsalted butter
3 egg yolks
2 tbsp lemon juice
Pepper, pinch of salt

*** An electric blender is needed to make hollandaise sauce this quick and easy way**

Put the yolks in the blender with the lemon juice, salt and pepper. Mix briefly. Melt the butter in a small saucepan and when it is bubbling, pour slowly on to the yolks with the blender running. The sauce should now be thick and ready to use.

This is a quick way of making a hollandaise sauce. The classic way is slow, is difficult to keep hot and tends to curdle, so I don`t recommend it!

HOT POT WITH SUET CRUST (3)*

1 tin stewed steak
2 onions, sliced
2 sticks celery, sliced
1 lb (450g) potatoes cut in chunks
8 oz (225g) carrots, sliced
Beef stock cube and water and, if available, some red wine
Seasoning, bay leaf and herbs

Topping: 4 oz (110g) self-raising flour
           2 oz (50g) shredded suet
           Little salt

This is a very good economical all-in-one-dish

Place sliced carrots in saucepan with stock cube, water to cover and flavouring. Bring to boil and simmer 15 minutes. Add potatoes, onions and celery and cook for 15 to 20 minutes. Add steak and more liquid to cover (if necessary) and cook for another 5 minutes. Put into pie dish. Mix flour and suet with very little water so that it will roll out. Place on top of the meat. Make hole in the middle. Cook in hot oven for about 25 minutes.

HUMMUS

Tin of chick peas
2 cloves garlic
Juice of 1 lemon
4 tbsp tahini
4 tbsp olive oil
Pinch of salt, cayenne and cumin
Chopped parsley or coriander

Drain the chick peas, keeping some of the liquid and put in a mixer with the cloves of garlic, crushed, the tahini paste and the juice of a lemon. Mix and then add the olive oil slowly. Add a pinch of salt, cayenne and cumin. Taste for seasoning and add more if necessary. Lastly add some chopped parsley or coriander and add a little liquid from the tin if too thick.

Serve with toast or biscuits and/or with crudities. Freeze whatever is left.

ICE CREAM – BANANA

5 Bananas
Juice of 2 lemons
3 oz (75g) caster sugar
5 fl oz (150 ml) milk
5 fl oz (150 ml) double cream

Mash the bananas and add the sugar and lemon juice.   Bring the milk to the boil, cool it and add to the bananas.   Whip the cream and fold it into the banana mixture.   Pour into a deep box or bowl and put it in the freezer.   When it starts to freeze, stir with a fork.   Put on the lid and leave in the freezer.   This ice cream seems to set very hard so put it in the fridge about an hour before serving.

ICE CREAM – BLACKCURRANT

8 oz (225g) blackcurrants
4 egg whites
10 fl oz (300 ml) double cream
4 oz (110g) caster sugar

Place blackcurrants with 4 tablespoons sugar in a basin over simmering water.   Cook for about 15 minutes.   Puree and sieve the fruit and cool.   Lightly whip the cream and beat the egg whites in a separate bowl until stiff.   Add the rest of the sugar to the blackcurrants and add to the cream, then fold in the egg whites with a metal spoon.   Put mixture into a soufflé dish and freeze.   Beat with a fork just before it hardens.   Return to the freezer until needed.   Serve with biscuits.

ICE CREAM – CARAMEL

Caramel:
    4 tbsp water
    4 tbsp granulated sugar

10 fl oz (300 ml) double cream
2 egg yolks

Put sugar and water in small thick saucepan and heat slowly until sugar is melted.   Bring to the boil and boil hard until it turns to dark brown.   Meanwhile beat the cream until starting to thicken and also beat the egg yolks.   Once the caramel is ready, take off the heat immediately and pour, beating hard, onto the egg yolks.   Quickly fold into the beaten cream, pour into a pudding basin with a lid and freeze.

Turn out by dipping basin into boiling water, put on serving plate, and return to the freezer until ready to serve.   This ice cream is good with biscuits or chocolate wafers.

ICE CREAM – COFFEE SURPRISE

3 eggs
6 oz (175g) caster sugar
Tbsp instant coffee powder
Tbsp hot water
1 pint (570 ml) double cream

Chocolate sauce:
    6 oz (175g) dark chocolate
    3 fl oz (75 ml) water
    Tbsp brandy
    2 oz (50g) unsalted butter
    4 oz (110g) icing sugar

Make chocolate sauce by putting broken pieces of chocolate, water and butter in saucepan. Stir over low heat until chocolate has melted. Stir in icing sugar and brandy over heat. Pour mixture into a bowl, cover and freeze for several hours.

Make ice cream by combining eggs and sugar in pan over saucepan of water, whisking over low heat until frothy and slightly thickened. Dissolve coffee in the hot water and add to the egg mixture. Cool. Whip the cream and fold into the coffee mixture. Pour into bowl, cover and freeze until almost set. Remove and beat until soft. Place some in base of a bowl with a lid or an old ice cream carton and then top with alternate spoonfuls of the frozen chocolate sauce and ice cream. Freeze.

ICE CREAM – VANILLA

4 egg whites
2 oz (50g) caster sugar
10 fl oz (300 ml) double cream
Tsp vanilla extract

Beat the egg whites until they are stiff and beat the cream slightly folding in the sugar and vanilla extract. Fold the egg whites carefully into the cream mixture and put into a pudding bowl and freeze. Stir with a fork just before it hardens and return to the freezer until needed.

Serve with fruit or a chocolate sauce.

ICED LEMON SLICE

2 oz (50g) ratafia or digestive biscuits
3 eggs
4 oz (110g) caster sugar (vanilla)*
2 lemons, rind and juice
½ pt (300 ml) double cream

2 pint loaf tin, cling film

*** Vanilla sugar is easily made by keeping vanilla pods in a jar of caster sugar**

Crush the biscuits and put them at the bottom of the loaf tin lined with cling film. Separate the eggs and whip the egg whites until firm. Fold in the sugar, a tablespoon at a time, until stiff. Whip the cream with the egg yolks and fold carefully into the whites, together with the grated rind and juice of the lemons. Pour this mixture on top of the crushed biscuits. Fold over the cling film and freeze.

About ten minutes before eating take out of the freezer and put in the fridge on a serving dish. Remove from the fridge at the start of the meal and serve in slices.

ICING - FONDANT

Tbsp liquid glucose*
2 lb (900g) icing sugar
Egg white

***Can be bought in chemists**

The quantities given here make plenty to ice the recipe given under Christmas Cake (cooked in an 8 inch cake tin). This is the easiest way of making icing if you have an electric mixer. Put the sugar, egg white and liquid glucose in the bowl and mix well till smooth. Knead by hand and roll out between sheets of greaseproof paper and cover the cake with it, pressing down with the rolling pin. Decorate.

ICING – ROYAL

2 lb (900g) icing sugar (or more)
4 egg whites
4 tsp lemon juice
2 tsp glycerine

To make Royal icing whisk the egg whites until they become frothy. Add sieved icing sugar a tablespoon at a time beating well. Beat in lemon juice and glycerine. Add little more sugar if necessary. Cover bowl with damp cloth. Spread over the cake and draw up in peaks with a fork.

To make icing for piping and decoration, beat an egg white and sieve in at least 12 oz (325g) icing sugar until very stiff.

IMPERIAL CHICKEN WITH RICE SALAD (8)

1 large fresh chicken*
Butter, onion and lemon
2 Bananas, apple and/or pear

Sauce:
    4 tbsp honey
    2 tbsp mango chutney
    2 tbsp tomato jam or chutney
    Heaped tsp curry powder
    4 fl oz (110 ml) white wine
    5 fl oz (150 ml) double cream, whipped
    5 fl oz (150 ml) mayonnaise

Or buy a ready cooked chicken

Put the onion inside the chicken, pour over the juice of a lemon, dot with pieces of butter and cook in a hot oven for about an hour and a half. Leave to cool.

Make the sauce by putting the honey, chutneys and curry powder in a small saucepan. Bring to the boil and then simmer for 20 mins. Add the wine and when cool add to the whipped cream and mayonnaise. Take the chicken off the bone and mix into the sauce together with pieces of banana and slices of apple and/or pear. Put on a large serving dish and surround with rice salad made as follows:

1 lb (450g) long grain rice
4 tbsp tarragon vinegar
3 tbsp olive oil
Salt, pepper and nutmeg
4 spring onions, sliced
2 sticks celery, chopped
2 tbsp sultanas
2 tbsp flaked almonds
Red pepper, sliced

Cook the rice in a large saucepan of boiling water for about 12 mins. Drain and pour over hot water. Fork up and toss with the vinegar and oil and seasoning. Add the onions, celery, sultanas and flaked almonds to the rice when cold and surround the chicken. Decorate with slices of red pepper.

KEBABS

Per person:
    4 oz (110g) rump steak cut into pieces
    Small onion, small tomato
    3 – 4 button mushrooms, stalks removed
    Pieces of green pepper
Marinade:
    2 tbsp soy sauce, 6 tbsp olive oil
    2 tbsp lemon juice, chopped clove garlic
    Tbsp cumin, tbsp chopped onion, black pepper
Sauce:
    Onion, chopped, clove garlic, crushed
    Small tin of tomato puree
    5 fl oz (150 ml) stock or wine
    Chilli sauce
    Small carton of sour cream or crème fraîche

Make marinade and leave pieces of steak in it for as long as possible or, if short of time, pour some French dressing over the steak. Cook the steak in oil, heated with a crushed clove of garlic. Remove and then place on skewers with the onions, tomatoes, pepper pieces and mushrooms. Put on a baking dish.

Make sauce by cooking onion, mushroom stalks and some crushed garlic in the cooking juices from the meat. Add tin of tomato puree, any available stock and/or wine and a few drops of chilli sauce. Finally add sour cream or crème fraîche.

Cook 2 oz (50g) rice per person and reheat in an ovenproof dish. Cook kebabs in hot oven for 10 – 15 minutes. Place on top of the rice and serve with the sauce. This can of course be cooked on a barbecue.

KEDGEREE (3 – 4)

1 lb (450g) smoked haddock
Milk to cover the fish
8 oz (225g) long grain rice
4 eggs
3 oz (75g) butter
5 fl oz (150 ml) crème fraîche or single cream
Handful parsley
Seasoning

Cook the haddock in milk. Cool and flake. Cook the rice in a large saucepan of boiling water for 12 minutes, then drain. Hard-boil the eggs for 10 minutes. Peel and chop. Chop the parsley finely. Melt the butter and mix in all the other ingredients, seasoning well. Put in a fireproof dish, cover with foil and heat in a moderate oven for half an hour. Serve with lemon quarters.

The advantage of this recipe is that is can be made in advance and then reheated.

KIDNEY CASSEROLE (4)

6 lambs kidneys*
8 oz (225g) chipolata sausages
2 medium sliced onions
2 oz (50g) butter, tbsp flour
15 fl oz (450 ml) beef stock and 5 fl oz (150 ml) red wine
Small tin tomato puree
8 oz (225g) sliced mushrooms
5 oz (150g) frozen peas

If possible buy fresh kidneys in their jackets – they taste nicer and are usually cheaper

Fry sliced onions in butter or dripping. Skin, core and slice the kidneys and fry until brown with the sausages. Take out and put in a casserole dish. Add flour to the frying pan, cook for a minute or two, add the tomato puree and liquid, bring to the boil stirring and pour over the kidneys and sausages in the casserole. Finally add the sliced mushrooms and frozen peas. Cover and cook for 1 hour in moderate oven. Serve with a green salad and either potatoes (new or baked) or rice.

KIPPER PÂTÉ

Packet kipper fillets
2 oz (50g) softened butter
Tsp Worcester sauce
Tbsp cream
Lemon juice, ground pepper

Simmer the kippers in the bag for 12 minutes. Soften the butter in a bowl and add the kippers and juice from the bag, but remove the kipper skin. Add a tablespoon of cream, a teaspoon of Worcester sauce and some ground pepper. Do not add salt. Beat all together and add some lemon juice. Put into small dishes and serve with Melba toast and a slice of lemon.

KUMQUATS WITH LEMONS

1 lb (450g) kumquats
4 lemons
10 fl oz (300 ml) white wine vinegar
1 lb (450g) caster sugar
Jars with metal lids

Rinse kumquats and lemons and slice as thinly as possible removing pips. Put the vinegar, caster sugar and 10 fl oz water into a saucepan and stir over low heat to dissolve the sugar. Simmer, then add the fruit. Bring to the boil and simmer gently for 15 – 20 minutes. Draw off the heat and cool. Put into jars and keep in a cool place. Serve with ham and/or turkey.

LAMB

8 lamb chops
2 carrots
2 courget
2
a
Garli
a
S

Fry chops for about 15 minutes. Transfer to a casserole dish. Add carrots, courgettes and o
in the frying pan, add to the casserole
dish. Add liquid and add to the casserole dish... oven with the lid
on for 1 hour. Se

LAMB JOINT

1 leg of lamb – ab
2 cloves of garlic,
Sprig of rosemary
Tbsp oil, salt and
Potatoes

Make slits in the l
roasting tin. Rub
them to the boil, d
oven (220º/425 F

Remove the joint
having poured off
veg with
wit

LAMB

1 la
4
8 la
Ha
Cu
2 t
Stock

Slice
tom
lay

LAMB NOISETTES (6)

12 noisettes
12 mushrooms
12 slices of thin bacon
2 tbsp butter
5 tbsp or more wine or stock
Shallot, garlic, seasoning

Cocktail sticks

Put a slice of bacon round each noisette and fix with a cocktail stick.   Cook in a frying pan with the butter.   Place in a flat casserole with a lid (or use foil).   Then fry some chopped shallot and crushed garlic and sliced mushrooms.   Dust in some flour and pour on a little liquid, wine if you have it. Season and pour over the noisettes. Place in a moderate oven for at least half an hour.

Serve with mashed or new potatoes and a green vegetable.

LAMB SHOULDER (STUFFED)

1 shoulder of lamb – boned
2 cloves garlic, thinly sliced
1 lb (450g) potatoes
Stuffing: 12 oz (325g) sausage meat
           Onion, finely chopped
           2 oz (50g) butter
           Grated rind of a lemon
           3 tbsp chopped walnuts
           Tsp dried thyme
           Egg
           3 oz (75g) breadcrumbs

Make the stuffing by frying the onion in the butter for about 5 minutes. Then add the sausage meat, the grated lemon rind, the chopped walnuts, herbs and seasoning.   Finally mix in the breadcrumbs and the beaten egg.   Leave to cool and then stuff the lamb and roll up and tie with string.   Insert the slivers of garlic in the meat.

Place on a rack in a roasting tin and put into a very hot oven (220C/425F/Gas 7) for about ten minutes, then reduce heat to 160C/325F/Gas 3.   Parboil the potatoes for 3 minutes and put round the joint in a little lard or dripping.   Cook for another hour and a half.   Remove the potatoes and the joint from the tin and keep warm in the serving dishes. Pour off some of the fat from the roasting tin.   Put the tin on the stove and add some flour mopping up the juices. Brown this well and then add liquid, either stock, and/or water or wine – whatever is available. Season and add a little Worcester sauce.   Pour into a gravy boat. Gravy should be fairly thin and not too highly seasoned.

This is a good way of cooking a shoulder of lamb as it goes further and carves easily.

LASAGNE (14)

Homemade lasagne (see under Pasta, page 141) or a packet of lasagne
Mince – double quantity (see under Mince, page 120)
White sauce:
    6 oz (175g) margarine or butter
    6 oz (175g) flour
    3 pints (1.7 litre) milk
    Grated nutmeg and seasoning
Topping:
    Grated cheese (Parmesan or Cheddar)

Cook the lasagne as instructed and leave to dry off.   Cook the mince and leave to cool.   Make a white sauce by melting the butter, stirring in the flour, cooking for a minute, then adding the milk over a low heat.   Gradually mix all together and when there are no lumps, bring to the boil, stirring well.   Add grated nutmeg and seasoning.

Take one or two flat ovenproof dishes and put in layers – meat, lasagne, meat, white sauce, lasagne, meat and white sauce. Top with grated cheese. This dish can be frozen, if necessary, at this stage.

Reheat in a hot to moderate oven for an hour at least, having defrosted it if it has been frozen. Can be turned down and left for longer. Serve hot with a salad.

LEEK

The nicest and easiest way of cooking leeks is to wash them well and then slice them and steam them for a short time – about 10 minutes.

LEEK AND POTATO SOUP

1 lb (450g) mashed potatoes
1½ lb (675g) leeks
Bunch of coriander
3 tbsp olive oil
2 pts (1.1 litre) chicken stock (stock cubes could be used)
2 – 3 tbsp cream and seasoning

Slice the leeks and put in a saucepan with the stock – or water and 2 stock cubes – and simmer with the lid on until just tender for about l5 minutes.   Strain off most of the liquid and work it into the mashed potatoes with a wooden spoon. Put leeks, coriander (keeping some back for garnishing) and olive oil with a little of the liquid into mixer or liquidiser and make a puree Add to the potato mixture, stir well and add any remaining liquid. Taste for seasoning, return to the saucepan and bring to the boil.

Serve hot or cold with a little more chopped coriander and some cream. This is a good way of using up left over mashed potato, which can be kept in the freezer.

LEEK TART

Pastry: 12 oz (335g) plain flour
Good 4 oz (110g) butter
Scant 2 oz (50g) lard
5 tbsp water
2 oz (50g) unsalted butter
4 leeks, trimmed and sliced
2 eggs
10 fl oz (300 ml) single cream
Salt, pepper, grated nutmeg
3 oz (75g) Gruyere cheese, grated

Make the pastry either in a mixer or by hand rubbing the fat into the flour and then mixing to a paste with the water. Leave in fridge for about half an hour. Meanwhile, melt the butter, add the sliced leeks and stew gently, taking care not to brown them, until soft. Leave to cool.

Roll out the pastry and put into a fireproof flan dish or tin with a removable bottom – about 10 inches (25 cm) in diameter – line with foil and baking beans or rice and bake blind in a moderate oven for 10 minutes. Whisk the eggs and cream together, add seasoning and stir in the leeks. Remove the flan from the oven, take off the foil and beans, and carefully pour in the leek mixture. Sprinkle with grated Gruyere cheese and bake 180C/350F/Gas 4 for 45 minutes or so until brown. Serve warm or cold with a salad.

LEEKS AND HAM (4)

6 leeks (or chicory could be used instead)
6 slices ham
2 oz (50g) butter or margarine
2 oz (50g) flour
1 pt (570 ml) milk
4 oz (110g) Cheddar cheese
2 tbsp Parmesan, grated
Black pepper
1 lb (450g) potatoes (white variety)
1 egg, 3 tbsp milk
Seasoning and knob of butter

Wash and steam the leeks (or chicory). Drain and when cool wrap slices of ham round each one. Put in a flat ovenproof dish. Melt the butter, add flour, mix in the milk over a low heat. Stir well until there are no lumps, then bring to the boil. Remove from the heat, but stir in the grated cheese at once. Add little ground black paper and taste for seasoning. Then pour over the ham slices.

Meanwhile cook the potatoes. Then mash and add a little milk, butter and a beaten egg. Mix well and then pipe or put round the edges of the dish. Dust grated Parmesan over the sauce. Put in a hot oven and serve when really hot. This is a good one-dish meal for supper and can be made ahead.

LEMON CAKE

4 oz (110g) soft margarine or soft butter
6 oz (175g) self-raising flour
6 oz (175g) caster sugar
2 eggs, 4 tbsp milk
1 lemon – grated zest and juice
3 heaped tbsp icing sugar

Heat oven to 180C/350F/Gas 4 and prepare a 2 lb loaf tin by buttering and flouring it. Put flour, margarine, caster sugar, eggs, milk and grated lemon zest in a mixer and mix briefly or beat well by hand. Pour into the tin and bake in the heated oven for 50 – 60 minutes, until a skewer comes out clean. Meanwhile mix the lemon juice with the sieved icing sugar. Remove the cake from the oven when cooked, loosening the edges of the cake carefully with a knife and pour the lemon juice mix over the top of the cake. Leave to cool in the tin before turning out. Serve with a fork.

LEMON CRUNCH PIE

10 oz (275g) digestive biscuits, crushed
4 oz (110g) melted butter or margarine
2 tbsp caster sugar
10 fl oz (300 ml) double cream
Large tin skimmed condensed milk
Zest and juice 3 – 4 lemons

Melt the butter and add the crushed biscuits and sugar. Press into a tin with a removable base or a large flan dish, about 10 inch (25 cm) in diameter. Cook for 8 minutes at 150C/300F/Gas 2. Remove and leave to cool. Meanwhile beat together the cream and condensed milk with the lemon zest and continue beating while slowly adding the lemon juice until very thick. Pour onto the biscuit base.

Leave overnight, preferably in the freezer. Turn out if made in a tin and place on a plate and keep in the fridge for about 3 hours before serving. This seems to be popular with men who are not usually very fond of puddings.

LEMON CURD

6 oz (175g) butter
2 lb (900g) granulated sugar
4 or more lemons
4 large eggs
3 x 1 lb jam jars with covers

In large heatproof bowl over simmering water melt the butter. Add the zest of 4 lemons and the sugar. Squeeze the juice from the lemons to make half a pint of juice and add this as well, stirring until the sugar is dissolved. Beat the eggs and add to the lemon mixture and stir until the mixture thickens to a custard consistency. While hot pour into the jars. Keep in a cool dark place.

LEMON CURD ROULADE

3 large egg whites
6 oz (175g) caster sugar
Tsp cornflour, tsp white wine vinegar
Filling: 7 fl oz (200 ml) double cream
          8 heaped tbsp lemon curd*

Swiss roll tin, lined with non-stick parchment paper

Rather than make the lemon curd use a jar such as " Duchy Originals"

Whip the egg whites until stiff and then add the caster sugar a tablespoon at a time until very stiff and shiny.   Whisk in the teaspoons of cornflour and wine vinegar.   Spread the meringue mixture across the lined tin.   Place in a pre-heated oven (325F/160C/Gas 3) for 20 mins or more until light brown and crisp. Leave to cool as long as possible.

Turn the meringue onto a cloth dusted with sugar. Whip the cream and spread over the meringue going right into the corners. Then spread over the lemon curd. Mark with the back of a knife about an inch from the top corner on both sides and roll up towards you.   Put the cloth firmly round the roulade and leave in the fridge until the next day or day after or freeze.

LEMON MERINGUE PIE

Pastry: 8 oz (225g) plain flour
          2 tbsp caster sugar
          4 oz (110g) butter
          Egg yolk and 2 – 3 tbsp water
Filling: 4 oz (110g) butter
          5 eggs
          Juice of 4 lemons
          4 oz (110g) caster sugar
Topping: 3 egg whites
          6 oz (175g) caster sugar

Preheat oven to 180C/350F/Gas 3.   Make the pastry either by putting the ingredients in a mixer or, if by hand, rubbing cut-up butter into flour and adding in egg and water to form a firm paste. Line a 10 inch (25 cm) or 9 inch (23 cm) flan ring with a removable bottom with the pastry, fill with foil or greaseproof paper and baking beans or rice. Bake blind for 10 – 15 minutes. Remove lining and return to oven for few minutes to firm the base.   Leave to cool. Turn oven to 220C/425F/Gas 7.

Meanwhile melt butter over boiling water. Add beaten eggs, lemon juice and sugar, turn down heat and whisk until mixture thickens being careful not to let it boil or get too hot. When smooth (if necessary sieve) pour into flan.   While cooling, whisk egg whites, until stiff, mix in sugar and pour on top of the lemon mixture.   Place in hot oven for about 15 minutes to brown.

Serve cold with pouring cream.

LEMON MOUSSE (6)

½ oz (10g) or 1 packet gelatine
3 tbsp water
8 oz (225g) caster sugar
3 large lemons
10 fl oz (300 ml) double cream
10 fl oz (300 ml) single cream

Topping: Ratafia biscuits

Put the water in a ramekin dish, sprinkle over the gelatine. Melt over hot water in a small saucepan. Mix the sugar with the grated rind and juice of the three lemons in a large deep bowl and stir in the single and double cream. Whisk until thick and light. This may take up to ten minutes. Then gradually whisk in the gelatine mixture and continue beating until it is beginning to set. Pour into an attractive glass bowl.

Leave in the fridge, but remove at least an hour before serving to avoid a "gelatine" taste. Top with small ratafia biscuits at the last moment.

LEMON REFRIGERATOR CAKE

4 oz (110g) unsalted butter
6 oz (175g) caster sugar
4 eggs – separated
Rind and juice 1 lemon
2 packets sponge fingers

10 fl oz (300 ml) double cream

Oblong tin or freezer type box with lid.

Cream butter and sugar really well until white and fluffy, in mixer if you have one. Mix in the eggs yolks, one at a time. Slowly add the lemon rind or zest and juice mixing very well, so that it does not curdle. If it should curdle, just carry on and don`t worry. Beat the egg whites and fold into the lemon cream.

Line box or tin with the sponge fingers in a flat layer sugar side down. Pour over half the mixture, then press on another layer of fingers. Spread over the rest of the mixture and top with sponge fingers. Cover with foil or the lid and put in the freezer.

Turn onto serving dish and fork over whipped cream. Serve from the freezer. Cover with the cream just before starting the meal.

LEMON SYLLABUB (6)

10 fl oz (300 ml) double cream
3 tbsp sherry or white wine
3 tbsp caster sugar
Juice 1 lemon

Grated rind 1 lemon – for decoration

Place lemon juice, cream, sugar and wine in a large mixing bowl.   Whip (for some time) until very thick and creamy.

Place in individual glasses and grate over some lemon rind. Serve with biscuits.

LEMON TART

Pastry:

   8 oz (225g) plain flour
   4 oz (110g) unsalted butter
   2 oz (50g) lard
   1 egg yolk, 2 tbsp water

Filling:

   3 lemons
   8 oz (225g) caster sugar
   15 fl oz (450 ml) double cream
   1 oz (25g) unsalted butter
   4 eggs

Make the pastry by mixing the butter and lard into the flour and adding the egg yolk mixed with the water.   Leave in fridge for a little while and then roll out onto 9 inch tin with removable base or flan dish and bake blind for 15 – 20 minutes in a moderate oven using foil and baking beans or rice, having placed the tin on a flat baking dish.   Remove from oven.

Meanwhile melt the butter, add the grated rind or zest from two of the lemons and juice from the 3 lemons together with the sugar. Whisk the eggs and slowly and carefully add them to the mixture and lastly pour in the double cream.   Spoon into the pastry case and return to the oven for 30 minutes or more until set.   Do not turn the oven up, but leave in a moderate oven until the tart is firm.

Delicious served with clotted cream or crème fraîche.

LIVER HOT POT * (4)

1 lb (450g) pig or ox liver
4 oz (110g) streaky bacon
Tin of tomato soup – condensed
2 carrots
2 onions
2 tbsp flour
Salt and pepper

*** An easy, healthy, inexpensive dish for people who like liver!**

Slice the liver, the carrots and onions and chop up the streaky bacon. Season the flour and toss the liver in it.   Put the liver and the bacon in a casserole dish with the sliced vegetables and cover with the tomato soup, adding a little water. Cook with the lid on in a moderate oven for at least an hour.

LIVER PÂTÉ

8 oz (225g) chicken livers
1½ lb (675g) butter
1 onion
1 clove garlic
Bay leaf, thyme and parsley
Salt and pepper

Cut up the chicken livers and remove all skin and fat.   Put into a casserole dish with the butter, cut into pieces, the onion, sliced, the garlic, chopped into tiny pieces, salt, pepper and a bay leaf, some thyme and pieces of parsley.   Put into oven (180C/350F/Gas 4) for 20 minutes.   At the end of this time, stir well and turn the oven up a little. Cook for another hour, keeping the casserole lid on all the time.

Remove from the oven, pour off some of the fat and put the rest of the ingredients in a mixer until smooth or put through a sieve.   Place in a loaf tin (if wanting to serve in slices with toast) or put into a serving bowl.   Smooth the top and pour on the reserved fat.   Decorate with a few bay leaves. Refrigerate overnight.

Can be frozen but better fresh and quick to make anyway. Can be used on cocktail biscuits as well as for a starter with toast.

LOBSTER NEWBURG (2 – 3)

1 medium size lobster*
1 oz (25g) butter
4 tbsp brandy/and or Madeira
Salt and pepper
1 oz (25g) butter
1 oz (25g) flour
5 fl oz (150 ml) fish stock
5 fl oz (150 ml) white wine
10 fl oz (300 ml) double cream
6 oz (175g) long grain rice

The best time for lobster is early spring or late autumn.

If the lobster is alive, plunge it straight into a large pan of boiling water, if necessary holding down the lobster with the lid – it will be killed instantly!   Cook for 20 minutes and then leave to cool. Otherwise buy a ready cooked lobster.

Remove the meat from the lobster shell. (The shell could be used in the prawn bisque recipe). Discard the intestine vein, the sack of grit from the head and the dead man`s fingers. Cut the meat into one inch square pieces.   Melt butter in a small pan and add the lobster meat and seasoning. Cook until the lobster turns a dark red and then add the brandy and/or Madeira. Make a sauce by melting the butter, adding the flour, cooking for a few minutes and then slowly pouring on the fish stock and white wine.   Stir with a hand whisk and when all the lumps have gone bring to the boil. Add this to the lobster, mix well and cook for about 5 minutes. Finally add the cream and reheat carefully.   Cook or reheat the rice and serve with the lobster.

LOBSTER VOL-AU-VENT (6)

12 vol-au-vent cases, either frozen or ready-made
1 cooked lobster or crayfish tail
1 large tin of lobster meat
1 oz (25g) butter, 1 oz (25g) flour
5 fl oz (150 ml) fish stock made from lobster and/or prawn shells
2 fl oz (50 ml) white wine, tbsp brandy
Seasoning, tsp paprika pepper and tsp tomato puree
2 tbsp double cream

Cook the vol-au-vent cases, if using frozen ones.   Remove the meat from the shells and make a strong fish stock boiling them for about 20 minutes just covered with water.   Melt the butter, add the flour, strain on the fish stock (keeping some back to thin the sauce if necessary) and add the wine and brandy and the paprika and tomato puree.   Stir well and slowly, removing all lumps, bring to the boil.   Then add the lobster meat cut into very small pieces.   Mix well, simmer for a minute or two and then remove from the heat. Add the cream, taste for seasoning and either pour into the hot vol-au-vent cases and serve or leave to cool.   If not serving immediately it is best to put cold sauce into cold vol-au-vent cases and reheat in a moderate oven for about 20 minutes.   If making for a party the lobster filling could be frozen for a short time.

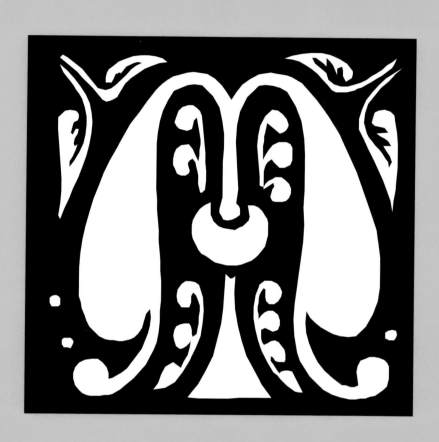

MACARONI WITH BEEF (4)

1 lb (450g) minced beef
1 tbsp oil
2 onions, chopped
Clove garlic, crushed
Heaped tbsp flour
Tbsp tomato puree
Small tin of tomatoes or 4 tomatoes (peeled and chopped)
5 fl oz (150 ml) stock (or water and/or wine with ½ beef stock cube)
Herbs and seasoning
8 oz (225g) macaroni

Topping: Knob of butter, tbsp flour
              5 fl oz (150 ml) milk
              Grated cheese

First make a meat sauce by browning chopped onions, garlic and meat in the oil. Then add flour and tomato puree, cook well and slowly add the liquid, tomatoes and herbs.   Bring to the boil, season well and simmer for about l5 minutes.   Meanwhile cook the macaroni in boiling water for about 8 minutes.   Drain and pour over boiling water.   Make a white sauce with a knob of butter, tablespoon flour and 5 fl oz (150 ml) milk, stirring until boiling so there are no lumps, removing from the heat and adding salt, pepper and grated nutmeg.   In a soufflé type dish or individual oven dishes put in the macaroni and meat in layers.   Finally pour over the white sauce and scatter with grated cheese.

Reheat for about 30 minutes.   Serve with a salad.   This recipe freezes well and should be defrosted before reheating for about one hour.

MACAROONS

2 egg whites
5 oz (150g) ground almonds
8 oz (225g) caster sugar
2 tsp water
Flaked almonds or whole almonds, peeled
Egg white for glaze

Rice paper

Mix the almonds, sugar and water together in a large bowl.   In a separate bowl beat the two egg whites until just stiff and then fold into the sugar mixture.   Put the rice paper onto baking sheets and pipe the mixture – or put out in small spoonfuls – onto the trays spaced well apart.   Press a flaked or halved almond onto each macaroon.   Brush with a little egg white and bake in moderate oven for 10 – 15 minutes until starting to colour.

If made small enough these are good served with puddings like syllabub.

MANGO CHUTNEY

12 oz (375g) dried mangoes*
8 oz (225g) brown sugar
2 inches (5 cm) ginger
2 cloves garlic
Handful raisins
2 small red chillies
Tsp salt, ground pepper
40 fl oz (1.1 litre) vinegar

3 x 1 lb jars with tops

These are sold in packets in supermarkets

Put the dried mangoes in a preserving pan. Grate the ginger, crush the garlic and add to the pan together with the sugar and raisins.   Remove the seeds from the chillies carefully and cut them into tiny pieces. Add to the pan with salt, ground pepper and the vinegar.   Bring to the boil and simmer for an hour or more until thick. Leave to cool down and then stir and put into the jars. Store in a dark cupboard and eat with curries.

MARMALADE – 4 FRUIT

3 lb (1.4 kg) fruit – 2 oranges, 2 grapefruit, 1 lime, 3 – 4 lemons*
6 lb (2.8 kg) sugar – preserving or granulated
5 pints water

10 x 1 lb jars with airtight tops lined with plastic

The fruit can be varied, but it is important for the total weight to be 3 lb.

Wash the fruit and cut in half. Squeeze out the juice and pour into a large preserving pan. Tie the pips in a small muslin cloth and add to the juice in the pan. Cut the fruit peels into quarters and slice into thin strips.   Add to the pan together with the water and bring to the boil. Reduce the heat and simmer for 1½ to 2 hours until peel is soft.

Remove the muslin bag and add the sugar.   Stir over low heat until sugar is dissolved. Boil rapidly until setting point is reached. Possibly after about ten minutes.   Start testing by putting a little in a saucer, putting in the freezer or fridge. When it wrinkles and forms a skin, when pushed with a finger, setting point has been reached. Take off the heat, leave to cool a little. Put into jars and cover with a lid while still hot.

This is my favourite recipe for marmalade as it can be made at any time of the year.

MARROW

2 lb (900g) marrow
3 oz (75g) butter or margarine
Seasoning
3 oz (75g) grated cheese

Peel the marrow and cut out the seeds. Cut into chunks. Sauté in the butter and season very generously. Put into a shallow fireproof dish and cover with the grated cheese. Heat in a hot oven for about 20 minutes or freeze and reheat.

MARROW CURRY

1 lb (450g) marrow
10 baby onions
4 red chillies
Tsp shrimp paste, tsp turmeric
Half inch fresh ginger
2 cups coconut milk
Tbsp oil

Cut up the onions and the chillies carefully removing the seeds (don`t lick your fingers!) and grind with the shrimp paste, the grated ginger and turmeric. Heat the oil in a frying pan and fry the ground ingredients. Add the coconut milk and bring to the boil, then add the marrow, cut into pieces with the skin and seeds removed. Simmer until tender for about 15 minutes and serve with rice and other curries.

MARZIPAN*

1 lb (450g) ground almonds
8 oz (225g) icing sugar
8 oz (225g) caster sugar
Tsp almond extract
2 egg yolks and small egg

Marzipan is very easy to make and so much nicer when home-made

Put almonds, icing sugar and caster sugar together either in a mixer or in a large bowl. Mix the eggs and almond extract together and quickly add to the dry ingredients to make a paste.

To use with a fruit cake, first brush the cake with a little heated sieved apricot jam and then roll or pat out the marzipan on top of the cake and press it all round the sides. Leave to dry for about three days before adding the icing. Keep any left over marzipan in a polythene bag and make into marzipan rounds using food colouring or make one of the following recipes – marzipan chocolate balls or marzipan dates.

MARZIPAN CHOCOLATE BALLS

Marzipan –see previous recipe
Small packet of chopped nuts
Tbsp Amaretto liqueur
6 oz (170g) dark chocolate, melted
Small packet of chopped almonds or hazelnuts
Icing sugar
Petits fours paper cases

Mix the marzipan with the chopped nuts and the liqueur and roll into balls.   Melt the chocolate over warm water.   Remove from the heat and dip the marzipan balls into the chocolate.   Then roll them in the nuts laid out on a baking tray.   Leave to cool.   Put into paper cases and keep in a tin in a cold place.

MARZIPAN DATES

Fresh dates
Marzipan – see recipe
Flaked or whole almonds, peeled
Caster sugar
Petits fours paper cases

Stone the dates and make a long slit in them.   Roll pieces of marzipan into small oblongs and stuff the dates. Press a flaked almond or a halved almond on top of the marzipan.   Roll the marzipan dates in caster sugar and place in a paper case.   You can, of course, colour the marzipan if you feel like it and also make some marzipan fruits.

MAYONNAISE

3 egg yolks
Tbsp wine vinegar or lemon juice
15 fl oz (450 ml) oil – mixture of groundnut or grapeseed and olive oil
Salt, pepper, little mustard.

Before making mayonnaise be sure to have the ingredients at room temperature. In a bowl mix the egg yolks with the vinegar and seasoning.   At first mix in the oil a drop at a time, beating well, then progress to a tablespoon and finally once the oil has started to thicken pour on the oil in a slow steady stream.   If it curdles, due to pouring the oil in too quickly, you can start again with another egg yolk, adding the curdled mixture very slowly.   If it is too thick by the time all the oil has been added, add a little more vinegar or lemon juice and/or if necessary some hot water.   Taste for seasoning.

If you prefer to make this in a mixer (not quite so good!) use one egg and one yolk.   This is fine for making a sauce like tartare sauce.

MEATBALLS

1 lb (450g) minced beef
8 oz (225g) sausage meat
Green pepper
2 cloves garlic
Tbsp parsley, seasoning
2 slices bread, 2 tbsp milk
Tomato sauce:
    Oil for frying, onion
    Dsp tomato puree
    Large tin tomatoes – 800g size
    2 – 3 tbsp wine or stock
    1 – 2 tbsp cream or crème fraîche
    Basil or other herbs as available

Soak the slices of bread in the milk.   Mix together the beef, sausage meat, half the green pepper, finely chopped, a large clove of crushed garlic, finely chopped parsley, the bread and some seasoning.   Form the mixture into balls – about 24 – and leave them in the fridge to harden a little.

Meanwhile make a sauce by frying the onion, chopped, the other half of the green pepper, finely chopped and another clove of crushed garlic, for about 5 minutes.   Then add the tomato puree, the tin of tomatoes and as available, some wine, stock and/or cream.   Bring to the boil and simmer for about 10 minutes.   Next roll the meatballs in seasoned flour and fry in oil in a frying pan.   Place in a casserole dish and pour over the sauce.   Cover and cook in a moderate oven for 45 minutes.   Remove the lid and cook for another 15 minutes.   Serve with noodles and green salad.

MELBA SAUCE

1 lb (450g) raspberries
5 tbsp icing sugar

Sift the icing sugar and sieve the raspberries in a plastic strainer into a large bowl.   Work the icing sugar into the raspberries with a wooden spoon until you have a thick cream.

Serve with a plain bombe or with peaches and cream or vanilla ice cream.

MELBA TOAST

Slices of white and/or brown bread

Toast sliced bread on both sides. Cut off the crusts and holding the bread down with the palm of your hand, cut through the centre of the slice. Turn over and now toast the soft centres of the bread under the grill or in a hot oven. Watch them carefully. Keep in an airtight tin. Serve with pâtés, cheese and soups.

MELON COCKTAIL (12)

Large melon or 2 ripe Ogen melons
4 grapefruit – ruby if possible
1 lb (450g) peeled prawns

Dressing:
    6 tbsp nut or olive oil
    2 tsp coarse grain mustard
    Tsp soft brown sugar
    ½ tsp salt and ground black pepper

Salad leaves
3 tbsp chopped mint – if available

Cut the melon flesh into balls. Leave to drain over a basin.   Cut segments of fruit from the grapefruit and also drain over a basin.   Add 2 tablespoons of the grapefruit juice to the oil and add the seasonings to make the dressing.   In a large bowl carefully mix the melon, grapefruit and prawns together and pour over the dressing.   Finally add the chopped mint.

Line some attractive individual bowls with a few salad leaves and carefully distribute the salad. Cover with cling foil and chill until needed.

MELON WITH BRANDY

Melon – as ripe as possible

4 tbsp brandy
4 oz (110g) icing sugar
Juice of l lemon

Buy the melon well in advance, so that it is really ripe.   Peel and cut into dice.   Put into an attractive glass bowl.   Mix the brandy and lemon juice and stir into the sieved icing sugar.   Pour over the melon pieces.   Cover with cling film and chill for at least two hours.

MELON WITH PARMA HAM (4)

One medium sized melon
12 slices Parma ham

Divide the melon into quarters.   Cut each quarter into two or three and put on individual plates. Leave the skin on but cut the flesh away from the skin and then slice downwards making fairly small pieces.   Carefully drape three thin slices of the Parma ham across the melon.   Cover with paper or cling film until ready to serve.

MERINGUE GATEAU

4 large egg whites
10 oz (275g) caster sugar

Filling: 10 fl oz (300 ml) double cream
        1 lb (450g) fresh strawberries or raspberries
          or:
        Small tin sweetened chestnut puree
        8 oz (225g) double cream
        2 oz (50g) plain chocolate
        Tbsp brandy

Non-stick parchment paper

Mark out in pencil three rounds approx. 8 inch (20 cm) each on parchment paper and place on baking sheets.   Turn the oven to its coolest setting.   Whip the egg whites in a large bowl, when stiff but not dry, whip in half the sugar with a metal spoon a tablespoon at a time.   When very stiff, fold in the rest of the sugar.   Spread equally over the three rounds.   Bake until firm.   This may take 2 hours or more.   If necessary change the positions in the ovens and turn them over.   Cool.

Fill the meringue layers with whipped cream and fresh fruit – if using strawberries it is best to slice them – or fill with a chestnut cream.   To make this, mix the puree with the brandy and then add the chocolate (melted over hot water) and the whipped cream.

MERINGUES

4 egg whites (not too fresh)
8 oz (225g) caster sugar (vanilla if possible)*

Baking sheets with non-stick parchment paper

Vanilla sugar is easily made by keeping one or two vanilla pods in a jar of caster sugar

Whip the egg whites in a large bowl until stiff.   Add half of the sugar, a tablespoon at a time and continue beating until very stiff – for about 5 minutes – even with an electric beater.   Then fold in the rest of the sugar with a metal spoon.   Either pipe or put out in spoonfuls on the parchment paper and cook in a low oven (100C/200F/Gas ½) for large ones for at least two hours until dried out. Small meringues, of course, will not take so long to cook.   If they start to brown turn oven down. They are ready when they are crisp on the top and firm on the bottom.   Keep in an airtight tin or freeze.

Large ones can be filled with whipped cream, whilst small ones are good to serve with fruit salads. They can also be served with Melba or chocolate sauce.

Egg whites from the freezer, defrosted, make very good meringues.

MILLE FEUILLE

1 lb (450g) puff pastry or packet frozen sheets of puff pastry
1 lb (450g) raspberries or strawberries or
     strawberry preserve
10 fl oz (300 ml) double cream
Icing sugar

Roll out the pastry onto two or three baking sheets as thinly as possible.   Prick all over and bake on wet baking sheets in a hot oven (200C/400F/Gas 6) for about 10 minutes until brown.   Turn over carefully and brown the other side if necessary.   Leave to cool.   Cut into 6 or 9 long pieces to make 3 layers.   Whip the cream and spread 4 or 6 of the pieces with jam and cream or cream and fruit. If using fruit, slice it so that it lies flat.   Make into two or 3 long strips, topping with a plain piece. Press down and dust with icing sugar.   Cut into individual slices, cutting slightly diagonally with care!   Put onto a long serving plate and leave in a cool place.

This is an impressive sweet – quick and fairly easy to make.

MINCE

1½ lb (675g) beef, minced
2 rashers streaky bacon
2 onions, 1 carrot
1 stick celery
Clove garlic, seasoning
2 oz (50g) fat or dripping
2 oz (50g) flour
2 tbsp tomato puree
8 fl oz (225 ml) water with beef stock cube
5 fl oz (150 ml) white (or red) wine
Tsp Worcester sauce

Chop the onions, carrot and bacon, slice the celery and crush the garlic.   Heat the fat in a saucepan and fry the vegetables until brown.   Add the mince and stir well until cooked and brown all over. Then add the flour and cook for 2 – 3 minutes.   Finally pour on the liquid, adding seasoning and Worcester sauce and the tomato puree.   Bring to the boil and simmer for at least 15 minutes, stirring occasionally.

Serve with spaghetti or gnocchi and a green salad.

MINCEMEAT

12 oz (335g) seedless raisins
8 oz (225g) sultanas
1 lb (450g) cooking apples
6 oz (175g) shredded suet
12 oz (335g) soft dark brown sugar
8 oz (225g) chopped mixed peel
4 oz (110g) chopped almonds
Grated rind and juice 2 large lemons
Tsp mixed spice
4 fl oz (110 ml) brandy

4 x 1 lb jars

Peel, core and chop the apples and mix with all the other dry ingredients.   Grate the rind from the lemon and then squeeze out the juice. Add this to the mixture followed by the brandy. Put into clean dry jars with airtight lids.

Leave up to 3 months, turning occasionally. Use to make either small or large mince pies.

MINCE PIES

1 lb (450g) mincemeat

Pastry: 12 oz (335g) plain flour
   8 oz (225g) unsalted butter
   3 oz (75g) ground almonds
   3 oz (75g) caster sugar
   2 egg yolks and 2 tbsp cold water
      or
   8 oz (225g) plain flour
   2 oz (50g) each lard and butter
   2 tbsp icing sugar
   2 tbsp water, tsp lemon juice and ½ tsp vanilla essence

Make the pastry or pastries by mixing the flour and sugars etc. and then adding the fats, until like breadcrumbs, followed by the liquids.   Leave in the fridge for about half an hour or longer.

Roll out and line small jam tart tins with the pastry.   Fill with heaped teaspoonfuls of mincemeat and then top with a smaller circle of pastry. Wet the edges of the pastry and press down well at the sides.   Cut a small slit or cross on the top of each pie, brush with milk or egg white and dust with caster sugar.   Bake in a moderate oven until starting to brown.

Keep in an airtight tin or freeze.   Reheat and serve – hot or cold – with brandy butter.

MINESTRONE

1 lb (450g) vegetables – e.g. carrot, onion, celery, parsnip, courgettes, potato
Handful of leaves from lettuce, cabbage etc or some green beans
Handful of broken spaghetti or macaroni
2 pts (1.1 litre) stock or water and stock cubes
Small tin of tomatoes or 4 tomatoes (skinned and chopped)
Tbsp tomato puree or ketchup
Seasoning and herbs as available
Oil, fat or dripping
Parmesan cheese

Chop all the vegetables into small cubes and cook in a large saucepan in fat for about five minutes without browning.   Then pour on the stock and add the shredded leaves etc, the pieces of spaghetti, herbs, seasoning, tomato puree, tomatoes and their juice.   Bring to the boil and simmer for about 30 minutes.   Serve with some grated Parmesan. Any soup left over can be liquidised and, with milk added, turned into vegetable soup.   Delicious and very simple.   Any vegetables can be used.

MINT SAUCE

Large handful of mint, tsp caster sugar
2 tbsp boiling water, 2 – 3 tbsp wine vinegar

Chop the mint finely and pound with the caster sugar in a small basin.   Pour over the boiling water and add wine vinegar.   Serve with lamb and keep any left over in an airtight jar.

MONKFISH (4)

1½ lb (675g) monkfish
2 large tomatoes
4 oz (110g) button mushrooms
Sauce: 2 shallots, finely chopped
            6 fl oz (175 ml) white wine
            Tbsp butter, tbsp flour
            Small clove garlic, crushed
            Tsp tomato puree
            10 fl oz (300 ml) fish stock
            Bay leaf, parsley, thyme

Make the sauce by simmering the shallots in the wine with the herbs until reduced by half. Melt the butter, add flour, cook a little and add crushed garlic, tomato puree and fish stock (this can be made from prawn shells or some fishy milk could be used). Add the reduced wine and cook until syrupy.   Cut the fish into slices and poach in wine or lemon juice and water together with some herbs, a bay leaf, peppercorns and a slice of onion.   Cook the mushrooms in a little butter. Drain fish, straining the liquid into the sauce. Place fish, tomatoes and mushrooms into a flat ovenproof dish. Pour over the sauce and reheat covered with foil in a moderate oven for about 20 minutes. Serve with rice.

MOULES MARINIERE

3 lb (1.4 kg) mussels
Onion or shallots
2 cloves garlic
Knob of butter
Thyme, bay leaf, parsley
7 fl oz (200 ml) wine
Seasoning

Brush the mussels and wash them very well in two or three changes of salted water, discarding any that are open and pulling off the beards. Put them in a large saucepan with some butter, chopped onion, crushed garlic and thyme, bay leaf and chopped parsley and the wine. Cover and put on a high heat for about 4 minutes.   During this time, hold on to the lid and toss them once or twice. Remove from the heat when most of them are open. Try to force open the others with a knife, but discard any that remain closed.   Tip into a large dish and pour over the sauce.   Grind some black pepper over them and divide into individual bowls.   Serve with French bread and finger bowls and have spare plates for the discarded shells.

MOUSSAKA (12)

3 lb (1.4 kg) minced beef
8 oz (225g) chicken livers
2 oz (50g) margarine
2 tbsp flour, 3 tbsp tomato puree
2 cloves garlic, seasoning
2 large onions
8 oz (225g) flat mushrooms
2 large aubergines
15 fl oz (450 ml) beef stock
10 fl oz (300 ml) red wine
Sauce for topping:
   1 oz (25g) butter
   1 oz (25g) flour
   1 pint (570 ml) milk – infused with mace, herbs, carrot, celery, onion and peppercorns
   3 oz (75g) grated cheese (Cheddar and little Parmesan)

Chop the onions and cook in the fat until golden brown. Add beef and chopped chicken livers and fry until browned.   Add sliced mushrooms and flour and cook for 1 – 2 minutes.   Then add the tomato puree, liquids, crushed garlic and seasoning. Stir until boiling, then turn heat down and simmer for 30 – 40 minutes.   Meanwhile slice the aubergines and fry or steam.   Make the mornay sauce by melting the butter, adding the flour, mixing well and then straining on a pint of infused milk.   Bring to the boil, stirring all the time, to avoid lumps, then add some grated cheese and season well with nutmeg and a little mustard as well as salt and pepper.   Place meat in large dish or dishes, cover with aubergine and top with the sauce. Sprinkle with Parmesan.   Reheat for about 40 minutes. This dish can be frozen. Defrost and then reheat in a moderate over for about one hour.

MUSHROOM SALAD

2 lb (900g) mushrooms
2 oz (50g) butter
2 tbsp olive oil
Seasoning
5 fl oz (150 ml) red wine
5 fl oz (150 ml) French dressing – see page 73

Cut mushrooms into quarters and sauté in butter and oil over a high heat for a short time. Turn down the heat and pour over the red wine, adding plenty of seasoning.   Boil until there is no liquid. Then take off the heat and mix in the French dressing.   Leave to get cold and keep in the fridge in a glass jar with an airtight lid.   Serve with cold meats.

MUSHROOM SOUP WITH RICE

8 oz (225g) flat mushrooms
2 onions
1 oz (25g) butter, 1 oz (25g) flour
2 pints (1.1 litre) chicken stock
Tbsp rice, seasonings
Bay leaf, parsley and mint

Slice the onions and mushrooms and soften in the butter in a saucepan with a lid on for about five minutes on a low heat. Add the flour, cook for one or two minutes, then pour on the stock. Stir until boiling and then add the rice, seasonings, bay leaf and chopped parsley and mint. Simmer for about 15 minutes.   Serve and garnish with little watercress or spring onion if available.

This is an unusual soup, quick and easy to make. Stock cubes could be used for the stock.

MUSHROOMS ON TOAST (2)

6 oz (175g) mushrooms
2 oz (50g) butter
1½ oz (35g) flour
5 fl oz (150 ml) single cream
Salt, pepper, nutmeg
2 large slices bread

Wipe and slice the mushrooms.   Cook in a small saucepan in the butter.   Remove the mushrooms. Add flour to the saucepan, cook 1 to 2 minutes, then stir in the cream together with flavourings. Return the mushrooms.   Keep hot while toasting and buttering the bread.   Pour mushrooms over the toast and eat at once.

NOODLES (4)

Packet of medium egg noodles

2 tbsp sesame oil
1 tbsp curry powder or curry paste
2 tbsp shallots
2 tbsp soy sauce*

*** Kikkoman is a good soy sauce**

Cook the noodles in a large saucepan for one minute.   Drain and leave to cool. Meanwhile chop the shallots and cook them in the sesame oil heated in a wok or large frying pan. Add the curry powder or, if preferred, curry paste and the soy sauce. Add the noodles and stir well over heat until really hot. Serve at once.

Noodles are very quick and easy to serve and make a change from rice or potatoes.

NOODLES WITH STIR FRY VEGETABLES (2)

4½ oz (125g) rice noodles
2 tbsp groundnut oil
Bunch spring onions
150g (5 oz) packet water chestnuts
Red pepper
150g (5 oz) bean sprouts
2 heaped tbsp tomato puree
2 tbsp soy sauce
2 tbsp sherry
5 tbsp water

Optional: handful of cooked prawns

Put the rice noodles into a saucepan and pour over boiling water.   Leave for five minutes and then drain and rinse in cold water. Drain well and leave.

Slice and shred the spring onions and water chestnuts. De-seed the red pepper and chop finely. Take sauté pan (or wok) and heat 2 tablespoons of groundnut oil.   Add the sliced spring onions and water chestnuts with the bean sprouts and red pepper. Cook over a high heat stirring well. Turn down a little and add the tomato puree, the soy sauce and the sherry together with the water. Finally add the noodles and prawns if using. Stir until really hot and serve at once.

NUT GATEAU*

6 large egg whites
9 oz (250g) caster sugar (vanilla)
7 oz (200g) ground almonds

Butter cream: 4 egg yolks
                  8 oz (225g) granulated sugar
                  ½ tsp vanilla extract
                  8 oz (225g) unsalted butter

Praline: 2 oz (50g) unblanched almonds
              2 oz (50g) caster sugar

Chocolate: 1 oz (25g) dark chocolate

8" (20 cm) cake tin with a loose base, cling film

*** Non-stick parchment paper is essential for this gateau**

Outline five 8" (20 cm) rounds from the base of the tin onto parchment paper and place on baking sheets.   Set oven to 350F/180C/Gas 4. Whisk egg whites until stiff but not dry and then fold in the sugar and ground almonds. Spread over the rounds.   Bake for about 20 mins turning over if necessary until lightly browned.   Cool.

Make praline by putting the caster sugar and almonds in their skins in a small saucepan and melting the sugar on a low heat.   If necessary stir with a metal spoon. Watch carefully and when dark brown pour at once onto a greased baking tin or sheet. Crush when set, ideally with a wooden hammer.

Make butter cream by mixing the egg yolks, sugar and vanilla in a blender for 3 minutes. Add the butter, cut into small pieces.   Remove half the mixture and add the crushed praline. Melt 1 oz (25g) chocolate on a plate over hot water and add to the mixture remaining in the blender.

To assemble the cake, line the cake tin with cling film and layer mixtures alternatively with the two creams, starting and ending with a meringue round. Leave in fridge. To serve, remove from tin, place on a large flat plate and decorate with strands of melted chocolate or grated chocolate.

Serve with some fruit, such as raspberries and/or blueberries and single cream.

OMELETTE (1)

2 large eggs
1 tbsp water
Salt and pepper
Knob of butter

Filling: Ham, mushrooms, shrimps and/or tomatoes
Topping: Grated cheese

Omelette pan*

To make a perfect omelette it is necessary to have a small thick frying pan, which is kept solely for omelettes and is just wiped over and never immersed in water

Lightly whip the eggs, add the water and seasoning.   Add a little butter to the pan and leave until really hot.   Pour in the mixture, stir briefly with a fork and when starting to set, lift up the edges with a palette knife to pour liquid from the middle to the edges.

Have some filling – chopped ham, sliced mushrooms and tomatoes with some butter or a pot of potted shrimps – heating up in a small saucepan.   Pour this onto the middle of the omelette, lift up one side to double it and then slide it on to a hot plate.   Cover with a little grated cheese – ideally Parmesan.   Eat at once. Serve with a salad and French bread.

OMELETTE ARNOLD BENNETT (2)

3 large eggs, little salt.
6 oz (175g) fillet of smoked haddock*
10 fl oz (300 ml) mixture of milk and water
Cayenne pepper, ground black pepper
3 fl oz (75g) double cream
1 oz (25g) butter
Grated Parmesan cheese

Large omelette pan

Be sure to buy the undyed smoked haddock

Put the fish in a shallow pan, cover with the milk and water, bring just up to the boil and then poach the fish for about ten minutes.   Drain the fish, removing any skin and bones.   Mix the fish with half of the cream and season with ground pepper and a pinch of cayenne.   Grate some Parmesan cheese. Preheat the grill.

Whisk the eggs with the rest of the cream, adding a little salt. Heat the omelette pan with the butter, pour in the eggs, tipping the pan up so that they reach the sides.   When starting to set add the fish to the centre and cook for a few more minutes.   Cover with some grated Parmesan and put the pan under the hot grill for one or two minutes until brown. Serve with extra Parmesan, a salad and some French bread.

ONION TART

Pastry: 4 oz (110g) plain flour
             3 oz (75g) butter
             Egg yolk and little water

Filling: 1½ lb (675g) onions
             2 oz (50g) butter and 2 tbsp olive oil
             2 eggs
             5 fl oz (150 ml) double cream
             Salt, pepper and grated nutmeg

Make the pastry by mixing the butter into the flour and adding egg yolk and little water to make a dough, which should not be wet.   Leave in fridge while preparing the filling.   Slice the onions and cook in a large saucepan in the butter and oil, without browning, for about half an hour until they are very soft and a pale gold.   Roll out the pastry and line a flan dish (not a loose-bottomed tin). Whip the eggs and add the cream and lots of seasoning.   Heat the oven to 200C/ 400F/Gas 6.   Put the flan dish onto a flat baking sheet.   Mix the egg mixture with the onions and pour into the flan dish.   Cook for about 35 minutes.

Serve warm with a green salad.

ORANGE CANDIED PEEL

5 large oranges
1½ lb (675g) granulated sugar – plus extra for sprinkling

Halve the fruit, squeeze out the juice and discard the flesh but not the pith.   Cut the peel into strips about half an inch wide (or less) and place in a saucepan.   Cover with boiling water and simmer for 5 mins.   Drain and repeat four times, using fresh water each time.

In a heavy pan put the sugar with 8 fl oz (225 ml) water and heat slowly to dissolve the sugar. When dissolved add the peel and cook slowly partially covered until soft (about 30 – 40 mins). Drain away any syrup and leave to cool.

Put sheets of greaseproof paper on baking sheets or Swiss roll tins and spread out the orange strips. Sprinkle well with caster sugar.   Leave in a warm place to dry for two or three days turning them in the sugar occasionally.   When dried keep in an airtight tin.

These can be dipped in melted chocolate if serving as a Petits Fours.

ORANGE CHUTNEY

3 large oranges
3 limes
3 clementines
2 large onions
1 large yellow pepper
8 large cloves garlic
2 fresh red chillies
Tsp turmeric, tsp salt
10 oz (275g) granulated sugar
10 fl oz (300 ml) white wine vinegar
10 fl oz (300 ml) unsweetened apple juice
10 cardamom pods, 6 cloves

Rinse fruit. Squeeze oranges and put into large saucepan or preserving pan. Cut peel into small pieces, discarding pips and pith.   Cut limes and clementines into eighths. Dice pepper and chop onions. Thinly slice the garlic and chop up chillies into very small pieces, being sure to remove all the seeds. (Do this with a knife, so as not to get them on your fingers). Crush the cardamom pods and put with the cloves in a muslin bag in the centre of the mixture.   Add all the remaining ingredients and bring to the boil. Simmer gently for one and a half hours, stirring occasionally until the mixture thickens. Remove muslin bag and leave to cool.   Stir and put into jam jars and cover with plastic airtight lids.

ORANGE SORBET (6)

6 large oranges and one extra for juice
Orange Curacao or Cointreau
6 oz (175g) granulated sugar
10 fl oz (300 ml) water
Lemon
2 egg whites

Cut a sliver off the bottom of six oranges so that they stand up. Cut a large slice off the top of each and squeeze out the juice and remove or press down all the pith making 6 cup containers. Grate rind from the lemon and extra orange and add to the juice. Then squeeze them and also add to the juice together with a drop of liqueur.   Make sure you have no more than 10 fl oz juice in total. Dissolve the sugar in the water over a low heat and when all the sugar crystals have melted, boil fast for 6 minutes.   Leave to cool and then add to the juice and freeze in an open container.

When mixture is starting to freeze, beat two egg whites and then whip the freezing mixture and fold in the egg whites. Return to the freezer.   A few hours later fill the orange cups and refreeze. Remove from the freezer half an hour before serving, but keep in the refrigerator.

The timing of this dish is quite tricky.

ORANGES WITH CARAMEL

6 – 8 oranges
3 oz (75g) granulated sugar
5 fl oz (150 ml) water
1 – 2 tbsp Calvados, brandy or orange liqueur

Topping:
    3 oz (75g) granulated or lump sugar
    3 fl oz (75 ml) water
    Handful of flaked almonds

Peel the oranges and cut some of the peel into thin strips.   Place in a small saucepan with the sugar and water. Melt the sugar over a low heat, stir and then bring to the boil.   Simmer until it thickens a little, take off the heat and add the Calvados, brandy or liqueur.   Leave to cool.   Meanwhile slice the oranges as thinly as possible and put in a fairly shallow glass bowl.   Pour over the syrup.

If time, make a caramel topping by melting the 3 oz sugar in the water slowly and then boiling it hard until it turns brown. Pour onto an oiled tin and when set, break into pieces, ideally with a wooden hammer.   Carefully brown the almonds in the oven.

Leave the oranges in the fridge and add the caramel pieces and the almonds at the last moment.

OXTAIL – BRAISED*

2 lb (900g) pieces of oxtail
Knob of fat
2 onions
2 carrots
3 sticks of celery
8 oz (225g) baby mushrooms
Heaped tbsp flour
1 pt (570 ml) stock or water and beef stock cube
Bay leaf, thyme, parsley
Seasoning

This dish benefits from being made the day before

Brown the oxtail in little lard or dripping in a flameproof casserole dish. Quarter the onions, peel the carrots and cut them and the celery stalks into strips. Add them together with the mushrooms to the meat and brown.   Add the flour, cook for a minute or two and then stir in the liquid, adding the chopped herbs, seasoning and a little wine if available. Put on the lid and transfer to a moderate oven and cook for at least two hours until the meat is falling off the bone. Leave to cool.   Remove the fat and replace in a clean casserole dish removing the bones.

Serve at once or reheat and serve with mashed or baked potatoes.

PANCAKES*

8 oz (225g) plain flour
2 tbsp oil
2 egg yolks
2 eggs
1 pint (570 ml) milk

Butter
Small crêpe pan

This quantity makes about 16 medium sized pancakes

Make the batter by hand or in a mixer. Put in all the flour with a pinch of salt for savoury pancakes and a pinch of sugar for sweet ones. Add 2 tablespoons of oil, 2 whole eggs, 2 egg yolks and half the milk (a mixture of milk and water could be used and if making sweet pancakes a tablespoon of liqueur could be added). Beat well and then add the rest of the liquid, stirring. Leave to stand. The mixture should resemble thin cream.

To cook the pancakes it is important to have a small thick crêpe pan (with a pouring lip) which is wiped over rather than washed up. Heat well with a little butter, pour in some liquid and pour away any excess back into the mixture. The first one will be too thick and should be discarded (or eaten!). Cook on both sides and stack. Pancakes freeze well if put between sheets of cling film.

Fill with various fillings – they too can be frozen either separately or in the pancakes.

PANCAKES – APPLE

Pancakes - 8 or more

2 lb Apples – Cox`s, Golden Delicious or similar
2 oz (50g) butter
3 oz (75g) soft brown sugar
Calvados (if available)
Topping:
    Knob of unsalted butter
    2 tbsp brown sugar

Make sweet pancakes including tablespoon of Calvados or other liqueur in the liquid. Make an apple puree by slicing the apples and cooking slowly over a low heat with the butter and sugar and a tablespoon of Calvados. Stir well until you have a puree. Leave to cool. Take a Pyrex or ovenproof plate or dish with a slight rim and make a cake with layers of pancakes and apple. Finish with a pancake on the top and shavings of butter and a little brown sugar.

Bake in a hot oven for 20 minutes or in a moderate oven for longer if covered with foil.

PANCAKES – CHEESE

8 or more savoury pancakes

2 oz (50g) Parma ham or equivalent
6 oz (175g) cheese (mixture of mozzarella, Gruyere, feta etc)
Small carton of crème fraîche
2 – 3 tbsp double cream
Seasoning, Parmesan cheese

Make pancakes, adding a pinch of salt.   Chop up some Parma ham and mix in a bowl with cubes of cheese. Add some crème fraîche and a little double cream until you have a firm mixture.   Season it well with salt, pepper, nutmeg and a little mustard. Put a tablespoon of the mixture in the middle of each pancake to make a parcel.   Put into an ovenproof dish and top with grated Parmesan.

Reheat in a hot oven until piping hot – about 20 to 30 minutes.   Serve with a salad or as a first course.

PANCAKES – HAM

Pancakes – 8 or more

2 oz (50g) butter
2 oz (50g) flour
Dsp tomato puree
10 fl oz (300 ml) liquid (milk, stock, little sherry etc.)
8 oz (225g) mushrooms,
1 lb (450g) ham*
Tbsp parsley, chopped
Tbsp cream.
Ground pepper
Parmesan cheese

This could include some cooked chicken

First make the pancakes.   Then chop up the ham – this could include some chicken – and slice the mushrooms.   Melt the butter in a small saucepan, cook the mushrooms, then add the flour and cook for a minute.   Then add the liquid gradually, leaving some behind.   Bring to the boil, stirring well so that there are no lumps.   Add the meat, the chopped parsley, some ground black pepper and the cream.   If very thick add a little more liquid. Fill the pancakes, roll up and place in a shallow fireproof dish.   Top with shavings of butter and some grated Parmesan.

Reheat in a low oven for 20 minutes. Serve with a salad. These freeze well.   Remove from the freezer about an hour before cooking.

PANCAKES – LEMON

Pancake batter with a little sugar
Lemons
Caster sugar

The pancakes should be freshly made. As you make them, stack them on a Pyrex or tin plate on top of a saucepan of simmering water and cover with a saucepan lid. Squeeze some lemons and when ready to serve put two pancakes on individual plates with a quarter of lemon. Pour over some lemon juice, double them up and shake over some caster sugar. Eat at once.

PANCAKES – PEACH

Pancake batter with some brandy added
Peaches
Sauce: Juice of orange
       Tbsp brandy
       2 – 3 tbsp brown sugar

Make the pancakes and pile up on a plate. Peel and chop some fresh peaches. Fill each pancake with some peaches and fold into square parcels. Put in a flat fireproof dish. Squeeze the juice from the orange and mix with the brandy and sugar. Pour over the pancakes and put in a hot oven to brown for about 10 – 15 minutes. Serve at once with thick cream.

PANCAKES – PRAWN

Pancake batter with a little salt
8 oz (225g) prawns in their shells
3 tomatoes
Onion
Tbsp cream
Knob of butter, tbsp flour
2 tbsp tomato chutney
Seasoning
Chopped parsley

Make the pancakes, adding a little salt to the batter. Any left over can be frozen.

Shell the prawns and put shells in a small saucepan covered with water and simmer for about 20 minutes. Drain and measure out 5 fl oz stock for the sauce. Peel, de-seed and chop the tomatoes and slice the onion. Cook the onion in the butter until soft, stir in the flour, cook a little and then add the liquid. Bring to the boil, stirring, remove from the heat and add the cream, parsley, prawns, tomatoes, chutney and seasoning. Leave to cool and then fill the pancakes, roll them up and put them in a flat ovenproof dish. Dot with butter and cook for about 20 minutes in a moderate oven. Serve with a salad and new potatoes. Do not freeze.

PANCAKES – SPINACH

8 Pancakes

1 lb (450g) fresh or 8 oz (225g) frozen spinach
1 tbsp cream, seasoning
2 oz (50g) mushrooms
2 oz (50g) butter

Sauce: 1½ oz (35g) butter
             1½ oz (35g) flour
             1 pint (570 ml) milk
             2 oz (50g) grated cheese (Gruyere or Cheddar)

Topping: Parmesan or grated Cheddar and little butter

Make the pancakes and cook the spinach, draining well and chopping if necessary. Add a knob of butter, tablespoon cream, salt, pepper and grated nutmeg. Slice the mushrooms and cook in a slice of butter. Make the sauce by melting the butter, adding the flour, cooking for a minute and then stirring in the milk. Bring to the boil carefully making sure there are no lumps. Add the grated cheese, the drained mushrooms and the spinach mixture, holding back some of the sauce to make sure it is not too runny to fill the pancakes. Then fill the pancakes, either in a roll or a parcel. Place in a shallow fireproof oven dish and top with a little more butter and grated cheese –Parmesan is ideal for this. Cook in a hot oven for 20 minutes. These freeze very well in which case cook from frozen for at least 30 minutes in a moderate oven.

PARSNIP SOUP

2 oz (50g) dripping or margarine
1 lb (450g) parsnips
Onion, clove garlic
1 oz (25g) flour
Tsp curry powder
2 pts (1.1 litre) beef stock or water and 2 stock cubes
5 fl oz (150 ml) single cream
Seasoning
Chives or parsley, chopped

Melt the fat in a large saucepan and add the onion, chopped, the parsnip, cut into pieces and the clove of garlic crushed and fry gently for about 10 minutes. Stir in the flour and the curry powder and cook for a minute or two and then add the stock and seasoning. Bring to the boil, stirring and then reduce the heat, cover and simmer gently for 20 to 30 minutes until the parsnip is tender. Sieve or put in a blender. Reheat, add the cream and taste for seasoning. Garnish with chopped chives or parsley.

Serve with croutons. These are made by frying or baking small cubes of bread. They can be frozen and then removed from the freezer when needed. Reheat briefly in a hot oven.

PARTRIDGE (3)

2 partridges*
2 oz (50g) butter and 2 tbsp nut oil
8 oz (225g) mushrooms
6 oz (175g) smoked streaky bacon
20 baby onions or shallots
2 carrots
3 fl oz (75 ml) Calvados
8 fl oz (225 ml) dry cider
10 fl oz (300 ml) double cream
Juice of ½ lemon
2 cloves garlic, green peppercorns, salt, herbs

In season September 1ˢᵗ – February 1ˢᵗ

Remove innards etc. from birds. Season and insert small knob of butter, some chopped mushroom stalks, few pieces of bacon and sprigs of herbs.   Close up using a cocktail stick or string.   Brown birds in a flameproof casserole in knob of butter and oil and then add the rest of the bacon and the onions.   Flame with the Calvados.   Add mushrooms, carrots, cut into sticks, crushed garlic, the innards, salt and a handful of green peppercorns.   Then add the cider and a few more herbs. Simmer for about 40 minutes adding some water if necessary.   Remove birds and vegetables and strain. Put meat (without the bones) and vegetables in oven dish.   Add cream to the pan and reduce.   Season and add lemon juice. Pour over the partridges.   Reheat.

PASTA DOUGH

12 oz (335g) "00" flour *
2 – 3 eggs, 2 – 3 egg yolks
Tbsp oil, tsp. salt

For Lasagne: 10 oz (275g) "00" Flour
                          2 Eggs
                          1½ tbsp olive oil
                          Handful of chopped spinach

This is an Italian flour used for pasta making which is now widely obtainable

It is not worth making pasta unless you have a mixer, a hand rolling machine and something to hang the pasta on – either a broomstick handle or a pasta hanging rack.   Mix all the ingredients quickly in the mixer, remove and press into a firm dough.   It must not be wet.   Leave to rest in the fridge for about 30 minutes.   Breaking the dough into pieces, run it through the machine starting at the widest setting and folding it over and running it through 2 or 3 times until a smooth rectangle is formed.   Then run it through the other settings until it is very thin and hang out.   Cut into short oblong pieces for Lasagne and into strips for tagliatelle and return it to the hanging rails or broom handle.   Bring a large saucepan of salted water with tablespoon oil to the boil.   Cook the pasta for a few minutes, drain and pour over cold water.   Hang out until needed or serve at once with sauce.

PAVLOVA

5 egg whites
1½ tsp white vinegar
10 oz (275g) caster sugar
2 tsp cornflour

Filling:
   10 fl oz (300 ml) double cream
   Fruit – strawberries, raspberries, passion fruit or slices of kiwi fruit and banana

Large baking sheet and non-stick parchment paper

Heat oven to 100C/200F/Gas ¼. Whisk egg whites until stiff, then gradually whisk in half of the sugar a tablespoon at a time having added the cornflour to the sugar. Beat until very smooth, add the vinegar and then fold in the rest of the sugar. Spread half the mixture in a large round, marked out on the paper on the baking sheet. Pop into the oven for a second while putting the remaining mixture into a piping bag (if you have one). Then pipe or spoon all round the edge making deep sides. Bake for 2 hours or more until the meringue lifts off the paper easily

If there is too much mixture make some small meringues, which freeze well or will keep in an airtight tin.

Fill the Pavlova with whipped cream and raspberries or strawberries. Slices of kiwi fruit and banana (dipped in lemon juice) is another good filling, particularly in the winter.

PEA SOUP

1 lb (450g) split green peas, soaked overnight
Ham bone or knuckle
2 sticks celery
2 leeks, 2 carrots
2 onions
Clove garlic, crushed
2 bay leaves
Black peppercorns
Parsley, chopped

Chop the carrots and onions and slice the celery and leeks. In a large saucepan put the ham bone and the drained split peas and all the other ingredients. Cover with water to fill the pan three-quarters full. Simmer on a low heat for about 3 hours. Remove the ham bone and serve the soup as it is or press it though a sieve, if you prefer a smooth soup. If too thick, add some milk and bring it to the boil. Taste for seasoning, adding some salt if necessary.

Serve with hot rolls.

PEACHES

See also: Pancakes

PEACHES IN BRANDY (4)

4 peaches
1 oz (25g) caster sugar
1 fl oz (25 ml) brandy
Juice of half a lemon
Toasted flaked almonds

Put the peaches in boiling water for a minute. Drain, cool, peel and remove the stones. Cut in 6 pieces each and place in a shallow glass bowl. Add the sugar, juice of half a lemon and the brandy. Scatter over some toasted flaked almonds. Cover with cling film and leave in the fridge. Serve with single cream.

PEACHES WITH CINNAMON

6 peaches
4 oz (110g) brown sugar
Tsp cinnamon

Peel, core and slice the peaches.   Arrange them in a flat ovenproof dish and cover with sugar mixed with the cinnamon.   Bake in a hot oven (200C/400F/Gas 6) for about 20 minutes until the sugar has melted.

PEARS IN RED WINE

2 lb (900g) dessert pears
5 fl oz (150 ml) water
4 oz (110g) granulated sugar
5 fl oz (150 ml) red wine

Put the sugar and water in a saucepan, melt the sugar slowly and then bring to the boil and simmer for 3 minutes.   Peel the pears with a potato peeler leaving on their stalks. Put them in the smallest saucepan, which will hold them standing upright. Pour on the syrup and the wine.   Put the lid on the pan and poach gently until soft for about 30 minutes. Lift the pears out of the pan and put into an attractive fireproof dish.   Boil the juice hard until it has reduced to half and then pour it over the pears.

Leave till cold but turn the pears occasionally so that they absorb as much of the syrup as possible. Serve cold with whipped cream. These can be frozen, but the pears and the juice should be frozen separately.

PEAS A LA FRANCAIS

l lb (450g) peas in their pods or 12 oz (335g) frozen petits pois
1 small lettuce or other greenery
6 spring onions
3 tbsp butter
3 tbsp water, 2 tsp sugar
Tsp salt, ground pepper
Tbsp chopped mint or parsley

Shell the peas if using fresh ones.   Shred the lettuce and chop the spring onions and parsley.   Put into a medium sized saucepan and cover with all the other ingredients.   Put a buttered paper (use the wrapper from a piece of butter) on the top, cover with the lid and cook on a low heat for about 20 minutes.

PEPPERS – STUFFED

2 large red peppers
2 large yellow peppers
8 oz (225g) minced beef
8 oz (225g) sausage meat
4 oz (110g) rice
4 oz (110g) mushrooms, sliced
Onion, chopped
2 oz (50g) pine nuts (or peanuts)

Tomato sauce or tin of chopped tomatoes with herbs and wine

Cut the tops off the peppers, remove the seeds and blanch in a pan of boiling water for a minute. Drain.   Fry the beef and the sausage meat (in a little oil if necessary) stirring until brown, then add the chopped onion, the sliced mushrooms and the nuts. Meanwhile cook the rice for 10 minutes in boiling water. Drain and add to the pan together with some seasoning.   Remove and leave to cool.

Stand the peppers upright in a deep dish, which will hold them standing up.   Fill with the stuffing and put on the tops.   Surround with a tomato sauce (if you have some in the freezer) or open a tin of chopped tomatoes and put this in the dish together with a little wine and some herbs.

Cook in a moderate oven for about an hour.

PESTO

2 large handfuls of basil leaves
3 cloves garlic, seasoning
2 oz (50g) pine nuts
3 oz (75g) Parmesan cheese*
Olive oil – about 3 fl oz (75 ml)

It is worth buying Parmesan cheese in a block rather than ready grated as it tastes so much better

Crush the garlic cloves and put in a mixer with the basil leaves. Mix briefly and then add grated Parmesan and some salt and pepper. Mix and pour in some olive oil slowly until you have a thick consistency. Keep in a jar in the fridge and use to add to pasta dishes and soup. Also freeze a small pot. This is a good way of using up a surplus of basil from the garden.

PHEASANT (6)

Brace of 2 young birds (hen and cock) larded *
2 oz (50g) dripping or butter
2 tbsp flour
Salt and pepper

Accompaniments: 8 oz (225g) fresh breadcrumbs
                                fried in 2 oz (50g) butter or margarine
                        Game chips
                        Bread sauce
                        Braised celery

In season October 1st – February 1st but often not in the shops until the middle of October

Wipe the birds well and ensure there is nothing left inside them. Put a nut of butter inside each bird. Heat the oven to 200C/400F/Gas 6 and cook for 55 minutes, basting well. Then dredge the breasts with the seasoned flour and baste again. Return to the oven to brown for about 5 minutes. Dish the birds and make gravy by tipping off some of the fat in the roasting pan. Put the pan on the top of the stove, shake in some flour, stir well until brown and then add liquid – some of the vegetable water and some wine or just water and a teaspoon of Worcester sauce. Bring to the boil, simmer, season and strain into a gravy boat.

Serve with fried breadcrumbs, game chips, bread sauce, braised celery and Brussels sprouts.

PHEASANT BREASTS (4)

4 pheasant breasts*
2 onions
Knob of butter, tbsp oil
½ pt (300 ml) double cream
2 tbsp Worcester sauce
2 tbsp mango chutney
Salt, paprika

*** If you have a brace of pheasants you can prepare these breasts yourself and use the rest of the pheasants to make a delicious Pheasant Soup**

Slice the onions and cook slowly in the butter and oil until they are caramelized. Put into a shallow fireproof dish and cover with the breasts. Mix the cream with the Worcester sauce, mango chutney and a little salt and pour over the breasts. Shake over a little paprika. Leave uncovered.

Pre-heat the oven to 180C/350/Gas 4. Cook for 20 minutes, then turn off the oven but leave for another ten minutes.

PHEASANT CASSEROLE (6)

1 large cock pheasant (or brace)*
4 oz (110g) butter or dripping
4 oz (110g) green bacon, chopped
4 oz (110g) diced carrots
4 oz (110g) diced celery
2 tbsp flour
½ bottle red wine (or mixture of wine and stock)
2 oz (50g) button mushrooms (or more)
6 oz (175g) button onions
Salt, pepper, lemon juice

***Towards the end of the season, pheasants are better casseroled**

Fry pheasant until lightly browned. Fry bacon and vegetables having removed pheasant and placed in a casserole. Add flour to the vegetables, cook for a minute, then add wine and stir while bringing to the boil. Then pour over the pheasant in the casserole. Add the mushrooms and onions. Cook, covered, for 1½ to 2 hours in a moderate oven. Remove and leave to cool.

Cut the wings and legs off the pheasant and carve the breasts. Place in a flat casserole dish with the sliced breasts in the centre, surrounded by the legs and wings. Place the vegetables in the centre and cover with the sauce, seasoning well. Either put on the lid or cover with foil. Reheat and serve with game chips and a green vegetable.

PHEASANT OR GAME SOUP

Carcass of pheasant and/or other game
Tbsp dripping or lard
2 onions
2 carrots
3 sticks celery
Herbs, 6 peppercorns
Large glass red wine
2 pts (1.1 litre) strong stock
1 oz (25g) butter
2 oz (50g) or more mushrooms
Tbsp flour, seasoning
Lemon juice
Redcurrant jelly

Slice the vegetables and brown in a tablespoon of fat in a large saucepan. Break up the carcasses and add to the pan with herbs, as available, peppercorns, wine and stock. Simmer for about 1½ hours. Then strain, pressing down on the strainer, and keeping some pieces of meat back.

Melt the butter in a saucepan, add some sliced mushrooms, cook and then add a tablespoon of flour. Cook for a minute and then pour on the strained liquid. Bring to the boil, return some sliced or chopped pieces of meat, add a teaspoon or more of the jelly and a squeeze of lemon juice and taste for seasoning.

PHEASANT – SIMPLE

Hen pheasant (for 3) or cock (for 4)
Large cooking apple, chopped
Sprig of thyme
Salt and pepper
Tbsp redcurrant jelly
Tbsp double cream

Wipe out the inside of the pheasant. Stuff it with the chopped apple, thyme and seasoning.
Put the pheasant in a small casserole, top with a buttered paper and cover with a lid. Preheat oven to 200C/400F/Gas 6 and cook the pheasant for 50 minutes.

Remove the pheasant and the apple. Put the pheasant on the serving dish to keep warm. Put the apples in a small saucepan and add the redcurrant jelly and the cream. Cook to a puree and serve as a sauce.

To make this an easy meal serve with Kettle or Cape Cod crisps and a salad – possibly watercress, chicory and orange or a green salad.

PHEASANTS WITH APPLE (2)

Brace of pheasants
10 oz (300 ml) pheasant stock or water
6 – 8 tbsp apple puree
4 tbsp Calvados
5 fl oz (150 ml) single cream

It is helpful for this dish to have some pheasant stock and some apple puree in the freezer. Otherwise make some apple puree by cooking about 3 apples with little water, butter and sugar and use water with some chopped herbs and flavourings if you haven`t any stock. Put pheasants in a roasting tin and surround with the liquid. Cook for an hour in a hot oven.

Remove pheasant and carve breasts and cut off legs and wings. Put in a flat ovenproof dish. Pour off a little fat and put tin on top of stove. Bring to the boil stirring, add 4 tablespoons of Calvados and boil for l minute. Stir in the apple and the cream. Taste for seasoning and pour over the pheasant. Cover and keep warm in a low oven, or leave to cool and then reheat in a hot oven.

This recipe is a good one to have in November, when pheasants are at their best.

PIPERADE (3)

6 eggs
12 oz (335g) tomatoes
2 red peppers or 2 tinned pimento
2 clove garlic, crushed
1 shallot, finely chopped
2 oz (50g) butter
Salt and ground pepper

Remove the skin from the tomatoes, by plunging first into boiling water and then into cold. Remove the seeds and core and chop. De-seed and core the red peppers, if using fresh ones and slice.

Cook the tomatoes, peppers, shallot and garlic in half of the butter in a frying or sauté pan until mushy. Beat the eggs and add to the tomato mixture with the rest of the butter and plenty of seasoning. Stir until they start to set and serve at once with some buttered toast or Melba toast.

PISSALALIDIERE

Pastry:
    8 oz (225 g) plain flour
    4 oz (110g) butter
    2 oz (50g) lard
    1 egg yolk, 2 tbsp cold water
Filling:
    4 tbsp olive oil
    2 large onions (thinly sliced)
    2 tsp French mustard
    6 – 8 tomatoes (skinned and sliced)
    Clove garlic, crushed
    14 – 16 anchovy fillets
    12 – 16 black olives stoned and halved
Topping:
    2 oz (50g) grated cheese – Gruyere or Parmesan
    Tbsp chopped basil

8" (20 cm) flan ring or loose bottomed tin

Mix the pastry by adding the fat to the flour until it resembles breadcrumbs and mixing it to a dough with the egg yolk and water. Leave in the fridge for at least half an hour.   Roll out and line a tin or flan ring on a baking sheet and chill.   Make the filling by cooking the onions slowly in two tablespoons of the oil for about 20 minutes until golden.   Spread the mustard over the pastry, spread on the onions and then cover with the tomato slices. Cover with the anchovy fillets (which have been soaked in a little milk and drained) and decorate with the halved olives.   Finally sprinkle over some chopped basil and the grated cheese.   Sprinkle over 2 tablespoons of olive oil.   Bake in a hot oven (200C/400F/Gas 6).

This is delicious on a picnic. It can also be served as a starter, served in slices. Ideally individual tarts would look better but they are a lot more trouble. It is also a good vegetarian dish.

PIZZA DOUGH

½ oz (10g) fresh yeast or heaped tsp. dried yeast*
Tsp sugar
Tbsp oil, 1 egg
4 fl oz (110 ml) milk or water
8 oz (225g) strong white flour, tsp salt

Fresh yeast is obtainable at the bread counter at some supermarkets and bakeries. (Fresh pizza dough can be bought in France at the supermarkets` bread counters).

Heat milk with teaspoon sugar and pour on to the yeast.   Leave for 10 minutes until frothy.   Then add to the flour and salt together with the oil and an egg.   Mix well – in a mixer if possible – until a smooth dough. Leave in a bowl in a warm place covered, until double in size.

PIZZA WITH ANCHOVIES

Pizza Dough – see previous recipe

Filling:
  Tbsp oil
  2 onions
  Clove garlic
  Basil and/or other herbs
  Tin of chopped tomatoes or 1 lb fresh tomatoes
  Tbsp tomato puree, seasoning

Topping:
  Mozzarella or Cheddar cheese
  Anchovies
  Black olives, pitted

Slice the onions and cook in the oil with the clove of garlic, crushed.   Add the tin of tomatoes or fresh tomatoes, skinned and chopped, together with the chopped herbs, tablespoon tomato puree and seasoning.   Cook till thick.   Roll out the dough on a large baking sheet to make a round or onto a rectangular tin with an edge to make pieces for cocktails.   Spread over the filling, add slices of mozzarella cheese or grated Cheddar cheese and then lay on thin strips of drained anchovy and pitted olives cut in half.   If making cocktail bits have strips of anchovies crossing each other with pieces of olive at each cross to make for easy cutting.

Leave pizza in warm place for 10 minutes and cook in a hot oven for 20 – 30 minutes being careful it does not burn.   If for serving with drinks, cut into small pieces and freeze, if necessary.

PLAICE (2)

2 fillets of plaice*
3 oz (75g) prawns
6 small mushrooms
2 large tomatoes
2 shallots
4 tbsp white wine
Lemon, seasoning

Sole can also be cooked this simple way

If the prawns are frozen, pour over a little lemon juice and leave to defrost.   Skin the fish and place in a flat ovenproof dish with a little butter.   Peel, de-seed and chop the tomatoes.   Chop the shallots finely and scatter over the fish.   Slice the mushrooms and add these to the fish together with the chopped tomatoes, the prawns and the lemon juice.   Add the wine and seasoning and a few dots of butter. Cover with foil.   Bake in a moderate oven for 20 minutes.   Serve with new potatoes and peas.

PLUM TART

Pastry:
  8 oz (225g) plain flour, 2 tbsp icing sugar
  4 oz (110g) mixture of lard and butter
  2 tbsp water, tsp lemon juice, ½ tsp vanilla essence
Filling:
  2 oz (50g) unsalted butter
  2 oz (50g) caster sugar
  Large egg, 2 oz (50g) ground almonds
  Tbsp flour, 1 tbsp Amaretto liqueur
Topping:
  1 lb (450g) ripe plums
  2 – 3 tbsp apricot glaze

10" (25 cm) – 9" (23 cm) flan tin with loose bottom or large flan dish

Make pastry by mixing fat into the flour and adding liquid to make a firm dough.   Leave in fridge while making the filling.   Put butter, sugar, ground almonds, flour, Amaretto and large egg in the mixer or a bowl and mix quickly.   Roll out the pastry, line the tin or dish and bake blind with foil and baking beans or rice in moderate oven for about 20 minutes.

Halve and stone the plums.   Make apricot glaze by heating some apricot jam with a little water and lemon juice and sieving.   Remove pastry from oven, pour in the filling and top with the plums facing upwards.   Bake in oven at 180C/350C/Gas 4 for 40 minutes or longer until the filling is set. Cool a little, then brush over the glaze and dust with icing sugar.   Turn out (if in a tin) and serve with whipped cream.

PORK CHOPS – CASSEROLED

One per person of the following:
  Pork chop
  Apple
  Onion
  Potato

  Sage, chopped

Fry the chops in a frying pan on both sides until brown – taking about 5 minutes.   Remove to a shallow casserole.   Slice the apples, onions and potatoes and fry in the pan adding a little butter and/or oil, if necessary, again taking about 5 minutes.   Remove and put on top of the chops. Season well, adding some chopped sage if you have it and cover with a little liquid – either stock, water and or/wine or cider.   Cover and cook in a moderate oven for about 45 minutes.

Serve with red cabbage.   This is a very easy one-dish meal.

PORK LEG – STUFFED

Leg of pork, with the bone removed *
1 lb (450g) potatoes
Stuffing:
    Small onion
    2 oz (50g) breadcrumbs
    3 oz (75g) dry roast peanuts or cashew nuts
    Cooking apple
    Stick of celery
    Knob of butter
    Chopped herbs, parsley etc.
    Seasoning, lemon juice

Ask the butcher to do this for you

Chop the onion, apple and celery and add the breadcrumbs, nuts, chopped herbs and seasoning. Melt the butter and pour over, mixing well. Put the stuffing inside the pork joint removing the bone (if the butcher has not done so). Place in a roasting tin and rub the skin over with oil to make sure of a good crackling. Put in a hot oven (200C/400F/Gas 6) for 30 minutes. Then surround the joint with some parboiled potatoes and turn the oven down to 180C/350F/Gas 4 and cook for another 1½ hours.

Remove the joint, keep warm, pour off some fat and put the roasting tin on the stove. Add some flour, brown well and then add liquid – vegetable water, wine etc – and boil to make thin gravy.

POTATO SALAD WITH SAUSAGES

1½ lb (675g) Jersey or waxy new potatoes
2 tbsp wine vinegar, 2 tbsp olive oil
1 red onion, ½ cucumber
3 stalks celery
5 tbsp mayonnaise
Tbsp Dijon mustard
4 eggs
4 or more frankfurters
Seasoning, 2 tbsp chopped parsley

Boil the eggs for 10 minutes, peel and leave in cold water. Cook the scrubbed potatoes in boiling salted water until tender. Drain. While hot mix with the vinegar, oil and seasoning. Slice the onion and the celery and peel, de-seed and cube the cucumber. Mix the mustard with the mayonnaise and combine with the vegetables. Lastly slice the eggs and the frankfurters and mix all together. Top with the chopped parsley. Refrigerate till needed.

I do not normally like potato salad but this is delicious!

POTATOES – JULIET

Large potatoes – red if possible
Vegetable oil for frying

Medium sized baking tin

Wash the potatoes but do not peel them – wipe them dry.   Half fill a baking tin with oil. Cut the potatoes in half lengthways and fit them cut side down in the oil so they are touching and fairly tight in the tin.   Cook in a hot oven for about 2 hours until they come away easily from the base of the tin.

This recipe was invented by a friend of mine and is a cross between baked and roast potatoes.

POTATOES – MASHED*

1½ lb (675g) potatoes – floury white ones, like King Edwards or Maris Piper
5 fl oz (150 ml) milk
Knob butter, salt and pepper

Any left-over mashed potato can be frozen and used for cottage pie etc (defrost, reheat in a saucepan to get rid of any water, add butter and seasoning)

Peel potatoes, cut in half, put into cold salted water and bring to the boil. Do not overcook. Heat the other ingredients in a small saucepan.   When the potatoes are soft, drain them, return them to the pan to dry off, mash with a potato masher and then pour in the heated milk. Beat well with a wooden spoon.   Serve at once.   You can add an egg to the mashed potato and put it in a fireproof dish in the oven if you do not want to serve them at once.   Alternatively, you can mash the potato, make it level and smooth and pour the hot milk on the top in a thin layer without mixing it in. Cover the saucepan and leave it on the side for 20 minutes before giving it a final beat.

POTATOES – NEW – BAKED

1 lb (450g) new potatoes
2 tbsp olive oil
Clove garlic, crushed
Salt and pepper

Scrub the potatoes.   Take a flameproof shallow dish and heat 2 tablespoons oil in it on the top of the stove.   Put in the potatoes and brown them stirring well.   Add the crushed garlic and the seasoning, put on a lid or foil and transfer to a moderate to hot oven.   Bake for one hour.

POTATOES NORMANDE

1½ lb (675g) potatoes
1 oz (25g) butter
l0 fl oz (300 ml) milk
Seasoning

Peel and thinly slice the potatoes. Arrange in layers in a flat ovenproof dish, overlapping. Dot with butter and seasoning between the layers.   Pour over the milk, add a few more bits of butter, more seasoning and a little grated nutmeg to the top.

Cook in a moderate to hot oven (190C/375F/Gas 5) for about an hour.

POTATOES - POMMES DAUPHINE

Potatoes:

  1 lb (450g) floury potatoes
  Knob of butter

Choux Pastry:

  2 oz (50g) butter
  5 fl oz (150 ml) water
  2 ½ oz (60g) plain flour
  2 small eggs

Deep fat pan with fat for frying

Thermometer, piping bag

Boil the potatoes.   Make choux pastry by putting the butter and water into a small pan and melting the butter, then bring to the boil.   Sieve the flour and shoot into the pan quickly off the heat.   Stir well with a wooden spoon and return to the heat for a moment or two.   Then beat in the eggs one at a time until the mixture is shiny.   When the potatoes are cooked, drain them and mash well with a potato masher. Add some pepper, salt, grated nutmeg and a knob of butter.   Add to the choux paste and mix well.   Put into a piping bag and heat the fat in the deep-fat pan to 165C. Drop in lengths of paste, cutting them off with a knife.   Increase the heat to 190C as they cook. Drain.

Either reheat in the oven or freeze.

POTATOES PROVENCALE

1½ lb (675g) potatoes
2 tbsp olive oil
2 tbsp butter
Onion
2 tbsp wholemeal flour
15 fl oz (450 ml) vegetable stock
5 fl oz (150 ml) dry white wine
2 cloves garlic
Herbs – parsley, sorrel etc.
Black pepper, salt

Heat the oven to 180C/350F/Gas 4.   Peel and boil the potatoes for 10 minutes.   Drain and slice.
Put in a shallow casserole dish.   Heat the fats in a frying pan and fry the onion until golden.   Stir in
the flour and fry for about 2 minutes.   Add the stock and wine and bring to the boil stirring well.
Add the crushed garlic, the seasoning and the chopped herbs.   Pour over the potatoes, cover with
the casserole lid and bake for an hour.   Remove the lid half way through the cooking.

This is a typical French country dish.   It goes well with sausages.

POTATOES WITH LEMON

2 lb (900g) potatoes – waxy variety
2 oz (50g) butter
Onion
Grated rind and juice of a lemon
2 tbsp or more chopped parsley
Salt and pepper

Peel the potatoes and cut into one inch cubes.   Cover with cold water and bring to the boil.   Simmer
for 5 minutes and then drain.   Melt butter in the empty pan, add onion, chopped finely, and cook in
the butter without browning.   Stir in the grated lemon rind and juice, the chopped parsley and the
salt and pepper.   Return the potatoes and toss until evenly coated.   Turn into a flat ovenproof dish.
Bake in a hot oven for at least 50 minutes until soft.

These potatoes can be prepared in advance to the baking stage.

PROFITEROLES (makes about 24)

4 oz (110g) butter
10 fl oz (300 ml) water
5 oz (150g) strong plain flour
4 eggs

Filling:
    10 fl oz (300 ml) double cream
    Zest of 1 orange
    Tbsp brandy or Cointreau

Topping:
    Chocolate Sauce - see page 46
                    or
    Caramel – 8 tbsp caster sugar, 2 tbsp water

Cut up the butter and add to the water in a small pan.   Melt the butter, sieve the flour and when the butter is melted and the water is coming up to the boil tip in the flour all at once.   Remove from the heat stirring well and return to the heat for a moment or two.   Leave to cool and beat in the eggs one at a time making sure the mixture is not too runny – 3 eggs may be enough.   Pipe out or put in spoonfuls on to wetted baking sheets in small rounds – about 24.   Put into a heated oven at 190C/375F/Gas 5 and turn up to 220C/425F/Gas 7.   Cook for 10 minutes, then reduce oven to 190C/375F/Gas 5 for at least another 15 to 20 minutes. They should be firm. Remove and leave to cool.

Fill with cream, whipped with a tablespoon of brandy and serve with a chocolate sauce.

Alternatively, fill with cream, orange zest and a tablespoon of Cointreau and dip tops in caramel made by melting the sugar and boiling until dark brown.   Remove from the heat and work quickly.

PRUNE AND BACON ROLLS*

24 large prunes
12 rashers streaky bacon

Cocktail sticks

Sometimes called Devils on Horseback

Pour boiling water over the prunes and leave to soak for about 6 hours.   Drain and remove the stones. Trim the rind from the bacon and cut each rasher in half.   Wrap the half rashers round the prunes and secure with cocktail sticks. Cook in a moderate oven for 20 minutes. Serve.

These are very good, but fairly messy, so small napkins will be needed.

QUAIL – ROASTED (2)

4 quail
1 small lemon
Sauce:
   2 tbsp honey, 2 tbsp oyster sauce
   Tbsp sesame oil, tbsp soy sauce
   2 tsp Dijon mustard. ground pepper and salt

Roll of wide foil

Set oven to 220C/425F/Gas 7. Wash the quail and put a quarter of a lemon inside each. Using a baking dish with sides put the quails inside a large double sheet of foil. Whisk the sauce ingredients together and pour over the quail inside the foil. Make into a loose but tight parcel. Cook for 20 mins and then open up the foil to brown the quail. Baste with the sauce and continue cooking for another 15 mins. Turn off the oven and leave for about 10 mins.

Serve the quail with the sauce and, for a quick meal, crisps and a salad or, alternatively, roast potatoes and a vegetable, such as red cabbage.

QUAIL – STUFFED (6)

12 Quail, boned*

Filling:
   4 oz (110g) rice
   5 bacon rashers, chopped
   2 onions, finely chopped
   2 cloves garlic, crushed
   14 spinach leaves, shredded
   4 oz (110g) pine nuts
   Few mushrooms
   Knob of butter
   Seasoning, stock, cream

You should be able to order these from a butcher as they are sold at Smithfield Market

Cook the rice. Make the stuffing by frying the bacon, onion and garlic in a little butter.   Add the shredded spinach leaves and stir over the heat. Then remove and add the pine nuts and the cooked rice. Leave to cool and then stuff the quail, closing any gaps – if necessary – with a cocktail stick. Place the stuffed quail in a baking tin and cook in a moderate oven for 40 minutes. Remove from the tin and keep warm. Put the tin on the stove, add a few sliced mushrooms, a little stock and/or wine and bring to the boil stirring well. Finally add some cream and pour over the quail. Serve with a platter of vegetables – potatoes, courgettes, carrots and sweet corn etc.

QUAILS`EGGS WITH HOLLANDAISE SAUCE (2)

2 large slices of bread
6 quails` eggs
6 tbsp Hollandaise sauce
Ground pepper

Put a flat dish or pan on the stove, fill with boiling water, a dash of vinegar and salt and bring to the boil. Toast the bread and remove the crusts. Place on individual plates. Heat the sauce on a low heat. Turn the boiling water to a simmer and poach the eggs. Once the whites are set (almost immediately), remove with a draining spoon onto some kitchen paper. Place three on each piece of toast and pour over the Hollandaise sauce. Sprinkle with ground pepper.

QUICHE LORRAINE

Pastry:
    12 oz (335g) plain flour
    Tsp salt
    4½ oz (120g) butter
    1½ oz (35g) lard
    5 tbsp cold water

Filling:
    2 oz (50g) butter
    3 large onions, sliced
    8 oz (225g) bacon pieces or chopped streaky bacon
    1 pt (570 ml) milk
    4 eggs and 4 yolks
    Salt, pepper
    Grated nutmeg

Topping:
    6 oz (175g) cheese – Cheddar and a little Parmesan

Large flan dish or loose bottomed flan tin, approx. 10" (25 cm)

Cut fat into small pieces and mix in with the flour and salt. Add the water and mix till a firm dough.   Leave in the fridge.   Slice the onions thinly and cook in the butter until soft.   Add the bacon pieces and continue cooking for about 5 minutes.   Whisk the eggs and pour on the milk and season with pepper, nutmeg and a little salt.

Roll out the pastry and line a large china flan dish or a loose bottomed flan tin, placed on a baking sheet.   Heat the oven to 190C/375F/Gas 5.   Grate the cheese.   Spread a layer of the onion and bacon mixture over the base of the flan.   Carefully pour on the milk and eggs.   Finally, spread over the cheese.   Cook in the oven until brown and set – about 30 minutes.

Serve hot or cold with a salad.

RASPBERRY BRÛLÉE

1½ lb (675g) frozen raspberries
10 fl oz (300 ml) double cream
Caster sugar

Shallow heatproof dish

Thaw the frozen raspberries for a short time. Beat the cream. Put the raspberries in a shallow heatproof dish, press flat and spread over the cream. Leave in the fridge overnight or as long as possible.

Remove from the fridge and sprinkle with caster sugar over the top and at the sides. Heat the grill to maximum and put the dish underneath, watching carefully. With an oven glove turn it as it caramelises or caramelise it with a blowtorch. Return to the fridge for at least an hour before serving.

RASPBERRY

1 packet chocolate
4 oz (110g) dark
3½ fl oz (100 ml)
4½ oz (125g) ra

*These can be

Melt the chocolate
leave to cool a little
onto the biscuit base

RASPBERRY WHIP (7-8)*

1 lb (450 g) raspberries
6 oz (175g) icing sugar
Juice of 1 lemon
2 oz (50g) caster sugar
5 fl oz (150 ml) double cream
9 fl oz (250 ml) Greek yoghourt

*This can also be made with strawberries

Keep back 4 oz (110g) raspberries and mix with the caster sugar. Put the rest of the raspberries in the magimix, or mash, add icing sugar and lemon juice and mix. Whip the cream, add the yoghourt and whip again. Stir in the fruit mixture and the sugared raspberries. Put into individual glasses and leave in the fridge. Serve with biscuits or small meringues.

RICE – SWEET AND SOUR

8 oz (225g) long grain rice
Yellow and red pepper
2 oz (50g) dried apricots
4 oz (110g) sweet corn
Bunch of spring onions
Radishes
4 oz (110g) nuts – pine or peanuts
Handful of sultanas
Herbs and seasoning
Watercress or lettuce
Dressing: 4 tbsp groundnut oil
              Tbsp wine vinegar
              Tsp lemon juice, tsp runny honey

Ring mould

First of all make the dressing by mixing the oil, vinegar, lemon juice and honey together. Then cook the rice in boiling water with a little salt and a dash of oil. Drain and pour over some hot water. Then add the dressing and stir well. Remove the seeds and cores from the peppers and chop into small cubes. Cut or chop the apricots into small pieces. Cook the sweet corn and slice the spring onions and the radishes. Add these to the rice with some chopped herbs, the nuts and a handful of sultanas. Taste for seasoning and press into a ring mould.

Leave overnight in the fridge. When needed, turn out and put watercress or other greenery in the centre. Serve with cold meats and hard-boiled eggs.

RICE WITH HAM (4)

8 oz (225g) long grain rice
8 oz (225g) cooked ham
2 onions
8 oz (225g) mushrooms
1 oz (25g) butter, tbsp oil
4 oz (110g) frozen peas
Lemon juice, salt, pepper

Cook the rice in boiling water for 12 minutes, drain and rinse with cold water. Peel and chop the onions and cook in a sauté or frying pan in the butter and oil. Remove when starting to brown to a casserole dish. Slice the mushrooms and fry them in the remaining fat. Chop up the ham and put in the casserole dish with the rice, forking it well. Then add the onions and the mushrooms. Finally add some peas from the freezer, stir well and add a large squeeze of lemon juice together with some seasoning. Cover with the lid and cook in a moderate oven for about an hour before serving.

This is an easy meal – all it needs to go with it is a salad. It is a good way of using up the last of a ham joint.

SALAD – GREEN

Lettuce
Watercress
Green pepper
Spring onions
Fennel and/or avocado

French Dressing:
    Tbsp wine vinegar
    Salt, sugar and Dijon mustard to taste
    3 tbsp oil (olive and/or groundnut)

Wash all the salad ingredients well. Break the lettuce in small pieces. Take the large stalks off the watercress, slice the spring onions and if using some green pepper, be sure to remove all the seeds, and slice into thin strips. Remove all the water in a salad spinner or cloth, put in a salad bowl and pour over the dressing, stirring well, just before eating the salad.

Any type of salad can, of course, be used as long as it is green. Herbs and sliced cucumber can also be added, but it is best to keep to four or five ingredients. A little chopped fennel and/or avocado (tossed in lemon juice to stop it going brown) adds interest.

SALAD – MIXED (10)

Iceberg lettuce
Green pepper, de-seeded
Cucumber
6 spring onions
6 radishes
3 tomatoes
Quarter of small red cabbage

Slice the iceberg, peel and remove the seeds from the cucumber and cut into dice. Slice the green pepper and the radishes very thinly. Cut the tomatoes into quarters. Mix the lettuce, cucumber and pepper and put in a large flat bowl. Slice the red cabbage very thinly and pile this in the centre. Surround it with the quarters of the tomatoes. Finally top with the sliced spring onions and radishes.

Serve as it is without any dressing.

Alternatively, put the different ingredients in a large hors d`oeuvres dish.

SALMON

Small salmon - weighing about 8 lb (3.6 kg)
Lemon juice, dill, butter, white wine

Large dish or baking dish
Large piece of foil
                    or
Large salmon
White wine, water
Carrot, onion, bay leaf, parsley, thyme
Peppercorns, 2 tbsp vinegar, salt

Fish kettle

For a small salmon (feeding up to 12 people) remove head and gut. Wash well. Put the fish on a large piece of foil, squeeze over some lemon juice, chopped dill, nuts of butter and a little white wine. Close foil tightly and put on a large baking dish with a lip, curling the fish round. Cook for at least 1 hour at 180C/350F/Gas 4. Remove from the oven and leave to get cold.

A larger fish will have to be cooked in a fish kettle. In the kettle put slices of carrot, onion, a few peppercorns, parsley, thyme, bay leaf, little salt and some water and wine to just cover the fish on the grid. Put the kettle on the stove and bring to the boil. Cover with the lid and simmer for 5 minutes. Remove from the heat and leave overnight. Skin the salmon, put on the plate and skin the other side. If brave, remove the centre bone!

SALMON MOUSSE

Small tin (213g) red salmon
5 fl oz (150 ml) mayonnaise
5 fl oz (150 ml) double cream
Half a cucumber
½ oz (12 g) packet of gelatine
3 tbsp fish stock, water and/or sherry

Cut about 5 slices of cucumber for decoration. Skin and de-seed the rest and cut into small cubes. Put on a chopping board and shake over some salt.

Soak the gelatine in a ramekin dish in 3 tbsp of fish stock or water and sherry till firm; then dissolve by putting the ramekin dish over hot water in a saucepan over a low heat. Drain the salmon from the tin, removing the bones carefully and flake into a bowl. Whip the cream lightly and add to the salmon with the mayonnaise. Drain and wash the cucumber, dry well with kitchen paper and add to the salmon mixture with some ground pepper and a squeeze of lemon juice. Now pour over the dissolved gelatine and mix carefully. Pour into an oiled mould and put in the fridge.

Decorate with the cucumber slices and serve with hot new potatoes and a salad.

SALMON STEAKS

Per person:

Salmon Steak
Squeeze of lemon juice
Pat of butter
Chopped parsley
Seasoning

Foil sheets*

These are very useful and are obtainable by mail order

Put each steak in the centre of a piece of foil. Squeeze on the lemon juice, a little chopped parsley, a little salt and ground pepper and a nut of butter. Make into individual parcels. Place on a large baking tray with a lip in a moderate oven (180C/350F/Gas 4) and cook for 25 minutes.

Serve with new potatoes (Jerseys, if possible) and petit pois.

SALT BEEF – SPICED

4 ½ lb (2 kg) joint of brisket *
Ground cloves, ground mace
Allspice, black pepper
Tbsp dried thyme
8 oz (225g) dark brown sugar
6 bay leaves
12 juniper berries

Large sheet of foil

 *Order the brisket from a butcher a week before you need it and ask him to salt it for you.

A week before cooking the salt brisket mix together ¼ teaspoon of each of the spices and the dried thyme.   Unroll the joint and smear it all over.   Leave for 24 hours in a covered earthenware dish.

The next day add the crushed juniper berries and the bay leaves and then turn the meat each day for 5 days. On the sixth day drain the joint and re-tie it tightly. Heat oven to 140C/275F/Gas 1 and roast the joint wrapped in two layers of foil for 4 – 5 hours.   Drain and wrap in fresh foil. Leave to cool under a heavy weight.

Serve cold in thin slices with salads, chutneys and baked potatoes or crisps.

SAUSAGE CASSEROLE (4)

1 lb (450g) chipolata sausages
1 lb (450g) potatoes, diced
1 lb (450g) carrots, cut in strips
8 oz (225g) sliced leeks or spring onions
Onion, sliced
Tbsp lard
Tin of Oxtail soup

Fry sausages with knob of lard in frying pan till brown. Transfer to a large casserole dish. Fry the prepared vegetables in the frying pan for a short time, stirring, and then add them to the casserole. Add the soup and stir with a wooden spoon.   Continue stirring until it comes up to the boil, then pour it over the sausages and vegetables. Cook for an hour in a moderate oven.

This recipe is a great favourite with children and is very easy to serve as it is complete in itself It does not freeze because of the potato, but I have never had any left anyway!

SAUSAGES IN BARBECUE SAUCE

1 lb (450g) pork sausages
2 tbsp vegetable oil
2 tbsp tomato ketchup
2 tsp mustard
Worcester sauce
Salt and pepper

Prick sausages and place in a flat ovenproof dish or tin.   Mix the other ingredients and pour over the sausages.   Leave for at least an hour turning once or twice. Bake in a hot oven for up to an hour until brown. Serve hot, but any left over are delicious cold.

SAUSAGE ROLLS (Makes 36 small ones)

3 sheets ready-rolled puff pastry
2 eggs
1½ lb (675g) sausage meat
Onion, clove garlic
3 oz (75g) breadcrumbs
4 tbsp chopped herbs, like parsley, thyme and sage
Ground black pepper, salt, nutmeg and pinch of ground cloves

Beat the eggs, cut the pastry sheets in half and brush the edges with some of the egg. Preheat the oven to 200C/400F/Gas 6. Chop the onion finely, crush the garlic and mix with the breadcrumbs, chopped herbs, seasoning and sausage meat. Put rolls of the mixture in the centre of the 6 pieces of pastry. Fold over the pastry, brush the overlapping join with the egg and put join down on baking sheets. Brush the top and cut into small pieces. Slash the tops and bake for 15 mins. Turn down the oven slightly and bake until puffed and golden. These can be reheated and freeze well.

SCALLOPS (2 - 3)

6 large fresh scallops or packet frozen scallops
6 oz (175g) streaky bacon, chopped
6 oz (175g) mushrooms, sliced
3 tbsp butter, 2 tbsp flour
3 fl oz (75 ml) white wine
9 fl oz (260 ml) milk with, if possible, little fish stock
2 tbsp cream, salt and pepper
3 tbsp cheese (Gruyere or Cheddar and little Parmesan)

Sauté the chopped bacon and sliced mushrooms in tablespoon of butter quickly. Drain and place in an ovenproof serving dish. Wash the scallops, cut up, if large, and put in boiling water for one minute. Drain well and add to the ovenproof dish. Make a sauce by melting 2 tablespoons butter, stirring in 2 tablespoons flour, mixing well and then adding the liquid. Be sure to stir well before bringing to the boil. Remove from heat and add the cream and 2 tablespoons of grated Cheddar and/or Gruyere cheese. Season, pour over the scallops and top with tablespoon of freshly grated Parmesan. Reheat in hot oven for 10 minutes.

This would serve 6 as a first course if served in individual dishes or scallop shells.

SCAMPI PROVENCALE (2)

1 lb (450g) Dublin Bay Prawns in their shells*
2 large tomatoes, skinned and cored
6 baby mushrooms

Sauce:
    2 shallots, finely chopped
    Knob of butter, tbsp flour
    Tsp tomato puree, crushed clove garlic
    4 fl oz (110 ml) white wine
    Tbsp chopped parsley, tbsp cream

These are expensive, but worth it for a special occasion

Peel the prawns and put the shells into a pint of water with parsley, slice of onion, thyme, bay leaf and peppercorns. Boil for 20 minutes, strain and measure out 10 fl oz. Freeze any extra stock. Make the sauce by melting the butter, cooking the shallots and crushed garlic and adding the flour and a teaspoon of tomato puree. Cook for a minute and pour on the reserved fish stock and the wine and bring to the boil. Simmer until reduced and syrupy. Put the fish in a shallow fireproof dish. Chop the tomatoes and add with the mushrooms. Add cream and parsley to the sauce, season and pour over the fish. Reheat in the oven for about 10 minutes and serve with rice.

SCONES

8 oz plain flour, tsp cream of tartar
½ tsp bicarbonate soda
3 oz (75g) margarine
3 oz (75g) caster sugar
Egg, 2 – 3 tbsp milk

Sift the flour, bicarbonate soda and cream of tartar into a bowl, add the sugar and rub in the fat. Beat the egg and add to the mixture together with the milk to make a non-sticky dough. Roll or pat out on a baking sheet with a large ring or make individual scones using a 2" cutter. Makes about ten. Cook in a pre-set oven at 200C/400F/Gas 6 for 20 minutes. Serve warm with butter and jam and (for a special treat) clotted cream.

SCRAMBLED EGGS WITH SMOKED SALMON (2)

6 eggs
2 oz (50g) butter,
5 fl oz (150 ml) cream, pepper
4 oz (110g) smoked salmon pieces

Beat the eggs with a little cream and add pepper to taste. Melt the butter in a small saucepan, stir in the egg mixture and when starting to set add the smoked salmon pieces and the rest of the cream. Taste for seasoning and serve at once with toast.

SEA BASS (2)

2 fillets sea bass, fresh or frozen
Olive oil
Lemon juice, seasoning and dried mixed herbs
3 large tomatoes
Red onion
Romano pepper
2 tbsp olive oil, tbsp balsamic vinegar
Salt and pepper

Wide foil

Turn the oven to 190C/375F/Gas 5. Skin the tomatoes by putting them in boiling water for a minute, then putting in cold water. Cut into quarters, slice the onion and de-seed the Romano pepper and cut into chunks. Put all in a small roasting tin with 2 tablespoons of olive oil, a tablespoon of balsamic vinegar and seasoning. Cook for about 30 minutes.

Wash and season the fillets of sea bass. Take a double sheet of foil and smear it with olive oil and a squeeze of lemon juice. Place the fillets in the foil, top with a few dried mixed herbs and close the parcel firmly. Put on a baking sheet and cook for 10 minutes. Serve directly onto hot plates on top of the tomato mixture. Plain boiled new potatoes are best, I think, with this dish.

SEA TROUT (4 - 6)

2 – 3 lb (900g – 1.4 kg) Sea trout*
5 fl oz (150 ml) red or white wine
2 tbsp water
Bay leaf
Dsp gelatine powder
Tbsp sherry, tbsp water
Tbsp white wine vinegar

Decoration:
   Cucumber
   Lemons
   Prawns in their shells

Wide foil

Known generally, but incorrectly, as salmon trout

Wash and gut the fish. Turn oven to 180C/350F/Gas 4 and put the fish in a large baking or fireproof dish.   If enough room leave on head and tail, otherwise remove.   Curl fish and pour over the wine, water, bay leaf, salt and pepper. Cover with foil. Bake until cooked – about an hour. Leave to cool.

Skin and put on a flat serving dish. Skin the other side.   Remove the central bone cutting it near the head and at the tail and then lifting it out carefully.   Press fish together and put slices of cucumber along the slit.   Dissolve the gelatine in tablespoon sherry and a tablespoon of water in a ramekin dish over hot water and strain the liquid from the tin into a small saucepan.   Add the dissolved gelatine and the vinegar. Bring to the boil and leave until almost set.   Coat the fish and cucumbers with the jelly. Decorate with prawns and lemons.

SHORTBREAD

6 oz (175g) unsalted butter
3½ oz (85g) caster sugar – vanilla * (optional)
6 oz (175g) plain flour
3 oz (75g) ground rice

This is easily made by keeping one or two vanilla pods in a jar of caster sugar

Mix the ingredients together – ideally in a mixer.   Leave in the fridge for about a quarter of an hour.   Roll or pat out into an oblong tin with sides. Prick all over and bake in a moderate oven for about 30 minutes until starting to colour.   Remove from the oven and sprinkle with caster sugar. Cut into strips and leave to cool. You can, of course, also make this into a round – ideally in a 9 inch (23 cm) loose-bottomed flan tin.

SHORTBREAD WITH CHOCOLATE

6 oz (175g) unsalted butter
3 oz (75g) caster sugar
9 oz (250g) plain flour
4 oz (110g) chopped nuts
4 oz (110g) chocolate drops

Cream butter and sugar well, then add sifted flour and the nuts and chocolate drops.   Place into an oblong or square tin, pressing down well.   Bake in a moderate oven (180F/350C/Gas 4) for 30 minutes until starting to brown and turning a golden colour.   Remove from oven, leave for a few moments and then cut into squares.   Leave to cool before removing from the tin.   A delicious very easy recipe!

SIMNEL CAKE – FOR EASTER

6 oz (175g) butter
6 oz (175g) caster sugar
6 oz (175g) plain flour
1 oz (25g) cornflour
Tsp baking powder
3 Eggs
6 oz (175g) sultanas or raisins
6 oz (175g) currants
4 oz (110g) glacé cherries, washed and halved
Grated rind of lemon and orange
2 tbsp candied lemon peel, chopped

1 lb (450g) marzipan
3 tbsp apricot jam and tbsp water for glaze

Deep 7" (18 cm) or 8" (20 cm) cake tin

Line and grease a deep 7 inch (18 cm) or 8" (20 cm) cake tin. Pre-set oven to 150C/300F/Gas 2. Sift the flours and cream butter and sugar in a large basin, beating well. Beat the eggs and add one at a time adding a tablespoon of flour after each egg. Fold in half of the flour and add the rest of the flour to the fruit and rinds and peel. Finally fold in the fruit mixture. Put half this mixture in the tin, smoothing the surface. Cut off a third of the marzipan and roll out a circle to put in the tin on top of the mixture. Press down and put remaining mixture on top. Smooth. Put tin on a baking sheet and bake for at least 2 ½ hours until skewer comes out clean from the top of the cake.

Cool in tin.   Turn out.   Brush top with the melted jam and water (sieved) and put another round of marzipan on top.   Put 11 marzipan balls round the top of the cake, colouring them yellow and green if you have time!

SKATE WITH CAPERS (2)

2 small fresh skate wings – about 7 oz (200g) each
2 tbsp flour, 3 oz (75g) butter and tbsp olive oil
Juice of a small lemon, tbsp capers
Parsley chopped, seasoning

Rinse the skate wings and dry thoroughly. Place flour on a large plate and season well. Dip the fish in the flour on both sides and shake off the excess.

Melt a slice of the butter in a large frying pan with the oil and fry the skate over a medium heat for about 5 mins on each side until the flesh is firm and white and the skin is golden. Transfer to warm plates, cover with foil and keep warm.   Return the pan to the heat and add the remaining butter. Cook until it turns brown and smells nutty but be careful not to burn it. Remove from the heat, stir in the lemon juice, the capers (rinsed and drained) and the chopped parsley and a little more seasoning.   Pour over the skate and serve immediately. New potatoes go well with this dish.

SMOKED DUCK WITH QUAILS` EGGS (4)

Lambs lettuce or other salad leaves
6 radishes
8 Quails` eggs, poached*
6 oz (175g) smoked duck
Small baguette
Olive oil, mixed dried herbs

Dressing: 5 fl oz (150 ml) groundnut oil
                   2 fl oz (50 ml) white wine vinegar
                   Tbsp maple syrup
                   Heaped tsp Dijon mustard, salt and pepper

Poaching the eggs avoids the difficult job of peeling them!

Wash the radishes and slice them. Cut part of the baguette into about 20 small pieces, put in a bowl and cover with olive oil and some dried herbs. Toss so that the bread is thinly covered and bake in a hot oven until brown (about 8 mins) on a roasting tray. Cut the duck into strips if the slices are large. Fill a frying pan with water, dash of vinegar and some salt and bring to the boil. Turn down and break the quails` eggs into it. Once the white is cooked, which will be almost immediately, take them out with a draining spoon and put in a fireproof dish.

Before serving heat the croutons and the eggs a little in a warm oven. Then toss the washed lettuce in the dressing and put on four individual plates.   Add the smoked duck, the radishes, the croutons and finally the quails` eggs.

SMOKED EEL SALAD (4)

6 oz (175g) smoked eel fillets
2 crisp eating apples
Handful of croutons – see page 57*
2 tbsp creamed horseradish
Tbsp crème fraîche
2 tbsp French dressing or
    tbsp lemon juice mixed with tbsp olive oil
Salad leaves – lambs lettuce, watercress etc.

It is a good idea to have a supply of these in the freezer

Cut the smoked eel into strips.   Make the dressing by mixing the horseradish with the cream and the French dressing (if you have some prepared) or tablespoon lemon juice and tablespoon olive oil. Taste for seasoning and carefully fold in the smoked eel.   On individual plates, put the salad leaves, with the smoked eel in the middle, surrounded by some slices of apple (do not peel) and the croutons. Serve at once with a piece of lemon with rolls or Melba toast.

SMOKED HADDOCK (2)

2 smoked haddock fillets*
Small packet frozen or 8 oz (225g) fresh spinach
Milk, butter
2 eggs, seasoning
Seasoning

Buy the naturally smoked haddock rather than the yellow dyed kind.

Cook the spinach with little water and butter in a small saucepan. Drain.   Poach the fillets in a mixture of milk and water with some seasoning for about 15 minutes with the lid on the pan. Poach the eggs. On individual plates place the spinach covered with the smoked haddock topped with the poached egg. Serve with rolls or toast.

SMOKED MUSSEL DIP

Tin smoked mussels
3 heaped tbsp good mayonnaise
2 oz (50g) chopped herbs (parsley and/or coriander etc)
Pinch salt, pepper, lemon juice

Drain the mussels and liquidise with the mayonnaise and about two handfuls of well chopped herbs.   Season to taste, adding a little lemon juice. Serve as a dip with crudities and crisps.

This dip is commonplace in South Africa, but I have never had it in England!

SMOKED OYSTER RISOTTO (2)

Tin smoked oysters
4 oz (110g) rice – long grain or Uncle Ben
2 tbsp oil, onion
Tsp turmeric with little water
1 pt (570 ml) fish stock
3 oz (75g) frozen prawns*
3 oz (75g) frozen peas
Small tin pimento
Seasoning

Defrost these adding the juice of half a lemon to bring out their flavour

Peel and slice the onion and cook until soft in the oil in a large frying pan. Stir in the rice and add a teaspoon of turmeric powder diluted with a little water. Bring the fish stock to the boil and pour about a quarter of it onto the rice. Stir and when the liquid has almost gone add more stock, a quarter of a pint at a time, until the rice is just cooked and almost dry.

Drain the pimentos, cut into strips and add to the rice together with the peas, prawns and the smoked oysters, well drained from the tin. Stir over the heat and add seasoning to taste.

Serve at once or keep hot in a casserole dish in a low oven.

SMOKED SALMON AND ASPARAGUS (4)

4 oz (110g) of smoked salmon
2 tins green asparagus
7 oz (200g) Philadelphia cheese
Cream or crème fraîche
Lemon juice
Seasoning

4 Ramekin dishes, cling film

Oil the ramekin dishes and line with cling film. Then line with slices of smoked salmon allowing them to hang over the edge. Spread a layer of the cream cheese over the salmon. Drain the tins of asparagus (keeping the juice) and put a layer of asparagus in each dish. Then add more cheese. Turn over the smoked salmon and cling film, press down and leave in the fridge. Make a sauce in the mixer with any left over asparagus, some juice, crème fraîche and lemon juice to taste. If necessary, add some seasoning.

To serve, turn out onto individual plates and spoon over the sauce at the last moment.

SMOKED SALMON MOUSSE (6 - 8)

8 oz (225g) smoked salmon slices
8 oz (225g) smoked salmon bits
5 fl oz (150 ml) fish stock or fish soup
Heaped tbsp cream cheese with garlic and herbs
Packet of gelatine diluted with wine or sherry
10 fl oz (300 ml) double cream
Juice of half a lemon
Dill, chopped, and black pepper

Loaf tin, cling film

Line a loaf tin with cling film. Then line the base and sides with the smoked salmon. Mix the smoked salmon bits, the fish stock, the cream cheese, the lemon juice and black pepper together – ideally in a mixer. Do not add any salt. Mix the gelatine in a ramekin dish with 2 – 3 tbsp of sherry or wine and stand in a basin of hot water over the heat to melt it. Add it to the fish mixture with the chopped dill and then put it in the tin. Turn over any pieces of smoked salmon with the cling film and leave in the fridge overnight.

To serve, remove from the tin and cut into slices. Put on individual plates with a piece of lemon and serve with Melba toast.

Any extra slices can be frozen in cling film for another time.

SMOKED SALMON PÂTÉ

4 oz (110g) smoked salmon bits
2 oz (50g) unsalted butter
Lemon juice
Black pepper

Lemon quarters

Put the smoked salmon bits in a processor and season well with some ground black pepper. Do not add salt. Then put the butter in a small saucepan over a low heat and when melted add to the processor. Mix briefly.

Put into small dishes and serve with toast for a starter or spread over mini Melba toasts or biscuits and serve with drinks. Decorate with pieces of lemon.

SMOKED SALMON TARTS (4)

Pastry: 6 oz (175g) plain flour
            2 oz (50g) butter
            1 oz (25g) lard
            3 tbsp water

2 oz (50g) smoked salmon
12 Quails' eggs
6 – 8 tbsp mayonnaise
Small jam tart or miniature tins

Make the pastry in magimix or by hand by mixing pieces of fat into the flour and adding water to make a paste. Chill in the fridge. Make 12 miniature tarts either in individual tins or in small jam tart tins. Roll out the pastry to fit the tins and if you have individual ones put another tin on top to hold down the pastry. Bake in a moderate oven for about 10 minutes making sure they do not burn. Cut the salmon into squares to fit the tarts. Boil the quails' eggs for 2 – 3 minutes, shell and keep in cold water.

To serve put the smoked salmon on the tarts and top each with an egg putting three on each plate for four people. Cover each egg with a little mayonnaise, which can be thinned with a little milk if necessary.

SMOKED SALMON TIMBALES (6)*

6 oz (175g) thin slices smoked salmon
6 oz (175g) taramasalata
5 fl oz (150ml) whipping cream
Juice of half a lemon
Black pepper
6 slices pumpernickel bread

Lemons to decorate

6 ramekin dishes, cling film

This is a very easy, though expensive first course, which can be made the day before

Oil and line the ramekin dishes with cling film. Line with the smoked salmon slices. Whip the cream and mix with the taramasalata and the lemon juice and season with the black pepper. Do not add salt. Put equal amounts into the six ramekin dishes and cover with the cling film. Leave in the fridge for at least 4 hours.

Put slices of pumpernickel bread on individual plates, spread with butter and put the contents of ramekin dishes on top. Serve with slices of lemon.

SMOKED TROUT MOUSSE (8)

4 large lemons
8 oz smoked trout (filleted)
10 fl oz (300 ml) milk flavoured with onion, carrot,
   bay leaf, mace, peppercorns
1½ tsp gelatine
1 oz (25g) butter, 2 tbsp flour
Tbsp creamed horseradish
6 tbsp whipping cream
Egg white
Chopped parsley

Cut the lemons in half lengthwise. Squeeze out the juice, measuring out 4 tablespoons. Remove all the flesh to make good cases and cut off a slice at the bottom so that they stand on the plates. Heat the milk slowly with the flavourings and leave to infuse. Put the gelatine and the four tbsp lemon juice in a ramekin dish over hot water and leave to dissolve. Melt the butter, add the flour, cook for a minute or two and then strain on the flavoured milk. Bring to the boil, stirring, to make a white sauce. Simmer for a minute or two, turn into a large bowl and stir in the melted gelatine. Cool. Flake the fish and whip the cream and the egg white. Fold the fish, the horseradish cream, the whipped cream and the egg white into the milk mixture. Spoon into the shells. Leave in fridge.

Chill for at least 4 hours or overnight and serve with Melba toast.

SMOKIES (8)

4 small Arbroath smokies, boned and flaked*
10 fl oz (300 ml) double cream and/or single cream
4 tomatoes
Black pepper
Grated Parmesan cheese

8 ovenproof ramekin dishes

You can buy these over the internet from Arbroath Fisheries

Bone and flake the Arbroath smokies. Peel the tomatoes, by dropping them into hot water for a minute or two, de-seed and core them and cut them into very small cubes. Pour a little of the double cream into each ramekin dish. Divide the fish between them placing it on top of the cream. Add the cubes of tomato and season with black pepper – do not salt. Pour over the rest of the cream. Top each dish with freshly grated Parmesan. Put the 8 dishes on a large baking sheet. Pre-heat the oven to 200C/400F/Gas 6 and cook for at least 20 minutes. Serve with rolls and butter or garlic bread.

These are always very hot when they come out of the oven, so beware!

SOLE (2)

Lemon sole - filleted and skinned*
2 oz (50g) butter
Tbsp flour
3 tomatoes
4 oz (110g) button mushrooms
Asparagus from a small tin or jar
Fish stock

Ask the fishmonger to do this and make sure he gives you the bones

First either take some fish stock from the freezer or make some from some prawn shells or, failing that, make some by boiling the bones from the filleted sole in water with some dry white wine, chopped shallot or onion, parsley, thyme, bay leaf and half a lemon for 20 minutes. Strain into a sauté pan and poach the fish in the stock for about 10 minutes.

Melt 1 oz (25g) butter in a small pan, stir in a tablespoon flour, cook and leave. Remove the fish and put in a flat fireproof dish. Strain the stock onto the roux, stir well and bring to the boil. Cook the mushrooms in 1 oz (25g) butter and add the tomatoes, skinned and chopped. Put on top of the fish, add some asparagus and pour over the sauce. Cover and reheat in a hot oven for 20 minutes. Serve with new potatoes.

SPAGHETTI BOLOGNESE (4)

1 lb (450g) spaghetti
Salt
Tbsp oil

Parmesan cheese – freshly grated

Bolognese Sauce – see under " Mince" – page 120

The easiest and most foolproof way of cooking spaghetti is to bring a large saucepan of water to the boil, adding a little salt and a tablespoon of oil   Put in the spaghetti, bring back to the boil and boil for 3 minutes. Then remove from the heat, put a cloth on the top and leave for 7 minutes. It will now be ready to serve and can just be drained and mixed with a sauce.

Make the Bolognese sauce (make as "Mince") mix with the spaghetti and toss with grated Parmesan.

 Serve with a salad and extra Parmesan.

SPAGHETTI CARBONARA (2)

6 oz (175g) spaghetti
6 rashers streaky bacon
5 fl oz (150 ml) dry white wine
Egg yolk, seasoning
5 tbsp double cream

Parmesan cheese, grated

Cook the spaghetti in a large pan of boiling salted water for about 10 minutes – test to see when it is ready. Drain and pour over hot water. Return the saucepan to the heat and cook the bacon rashers, which have been chopped. Add some ground black pepper and the wine and return the spaghetti to the pan. Reheat gently and then add the egg yolk mixed with the cream. Take off the heat, toss the spaghetti and add some grated Parmesan. Serve at once.

SPAGHETTI WITH HAM (4 – 6)

1 lb (450g) spaghetti
8 oz (225g) cooked ham
Onion
Knob of butter,
Tbsp olive oil
14 oz (335g) tin chopped tomatoes (with basil)

Topping:
    3 oz (75g) white breadcrumbs
    3 oz (75g) grated parmesan

Chop the onion and fry it in the butter and oil and then add the tin of chopped tomatoes. Simmer for about 15 minutes. Cook the spaghetti in a large pan of boiling salted water with a dash of oil for about 10 minutes until tender. Chop the ham into small cubes. Drain the spaghetti and mix it with the tomato sauce. Add the ham and some black pepper.   Put into an ovenproof soufflé type dish. Mix the cheese with the breadcrumbs and put on top of the spaghetti with a few slivers of butter.

Either grill, if serving at once, or reheat later for up to an hour in a moderate oven. A green salad goes well with this.

SPELT BREAD

1½ oz (35g) fresh yeast*
15 fl oz (450 ml) warm water
1 lb (450g) spelt flour, tbsp salt
11 oz (310g) plain strong flour
Egg, sesame or poppy seeds

Miniature loaf tins (optional)

Fresh yeast can be obtained from the bread counter at some supermarkets and bakeries

Mix the yeast with 4 tbsp warm water in a large bowl. Add 2 tbsp of the plain flour and stir to a paste. Leave covered in a warm place for about 20 mins. Stir in the rest of the water, followed by the flours and salt. Mix and either put into a magimix for a few minutes or knead by hand. Return to the bowl and leave covered until well risen for about an hour.

Divide the bread into three. Form one piece into a long baguette and put on a greased baking sheet. Cut the other piece into rolls and the third piece put into individual loaf tins if available or make more rolls. Put onto another greased baking sheet. Leave to rise in a warm place. Brush with beaten egg and add sesame seeds to some of the rolls. Cook at 200C/400F/Gas 6 for about 20 mins until they come off the tins easily. These freeze well and can be reheated.

SPINACH CREAM (4)

1 lb (450g) spinach leaves
salt, pepper and nutmeg
4 tbsp crème fraîche
Butter, seasoning

Wash the spinach and put in a large saucepan with some salt. Cook slowly and when it has collapsed, drain it well, pressing it down to get rid of all the water.   Either chop it finely or puree it in a magimix. Add the crème fraîche, butter and plenty of salt, pepper and grated nutmeg.   Put in a shallow fireproof dish, cover with foil and reheat in a moderate oven for about half an hour.

SPINACH SOUP

1 lb (450g) frozen spinach puree
1½ oz (35g) butter, 1½ oz flour
1½ pts (900 ml) milk, infused with mace, onion, peppercorns etc
Tbsp crème fraîche, seasoning

Defrost the spinach and drain. Infuse the milk by putting in a saucepan with flavourings and bringing up to the boil.   Put on the lid, turn off the heat and leave for about 15 minutes.   Melt the butter, add the flour, cook for a minute or two, strain on the milk and bring to the boil, stirring well. Whisk in the spinach and add salt, pepper, grated nutmeg to taste and the crème fraîche.

SPONGE CAKE WITH ORANGE

6 oz (175g) soft margarine or soft butter
6 oz (175g) caster sugar
3 large eggs
Grated rind of 1 orange
6 oz (175g) self-raising flour
1 tsp baking powder
Filling: 3 oz (75g) unsalted butter, softened
           9 oz (250g) icing sugar, sieved
           3 tbsp orange juice
Icing: 3 oz (75g) or more icing sugar
           Tbsp orange juice, few drops of orange colouring

2 x 8" (20 cm) sandwich tins

Preheat the oven to 180C/350F/Gas 4.   Oil the sandwich tins and put a circle of greaseproof paper on the bottom. Mix all the cake ingredients together – either in a mixer or in a large bowl – until you have a pouring consistency.   Do not over-beat.   Divide the mixture between the tins and spread it flat. Bake in the pre-heated oven for 25 to 35 minutes until it has come away from the sides and an inserted skewer comes out clean.

Meanwhile mix the ingredients for the filling. Turn out the cakes on to a rack, leave to cool and then fill with the butter cream. Dust the top of the cake with icing sugar or make orange icing by mixing a tablespoon of orange juice with 3 oz (75g) or more sieved icing sugar and a little orange colouring.   Beat and pour over the cake.

SPONGE MARBLED CAKE

6 oz (175g) soft margarine or soft butter
6 oz (175g) caster sugar
2 eggs
8 oz (225g) self-raising flour
2 tbsp cocoa powder
Topping: 4 oz (110g) unsalted butter
           Small packet of chocolate chips
           Small egg
           14 oz (400g) icing sugar

Deep cake tin – 7" or 8" (18 – 20 cm)

Pre-heat the oven to 180C/350F/Gas 4 and grease and line the cake tin.   Mix the margarine, caster sugar, eggs and flour together well – either in a mixer or using a beater. Add the cocoa with 2 tbsp hot water.   Divide the cake mixture in half and add the cocoa liquid to one half.   Put large spoonfuls of the mixture alternatively in the tin and then quickly smooth down. Bake in the oven for about 1½ hours testing with a skewer.   Leave to cool in the tin, then turn out on to a wire rack. Meanwhile make the topping by melting the chocolate and butter over hot water. When melted mix in the beaten egg, remove from heat and sieve in the icing sugar. Spread over top and sides of cake.

STEAK AND KIDNEY PIE (6)

2 lb (900g) stewing steak
8 oz (225g) ox kidney
3 tbsp flour, seasoning
3 tbsp chopped parsley,
1 onion, finely chopped
1 pint (570 ml) beef stock (or water and stock cube)
8 oz (225g) puff pastry (frozen or ready-made)
Small egg, salt

Cut the steak into small cubes and the kidney into tiny pieces, removing the core and skin. Toss the meat in the flour, which has been seasoned and put it in a casserole dish, layering it with the finely chopped onion and parsley. Pour over the stock (or water mixed with a stock cube) to cover. Cook in a moderate oven for two hours. Leave to cool.

Remove any fat, which has risen to the surface. Put in a pie dish with a pie funnel. Roll out the pastry and put a strip round the edge of the pie dish. Brush with water and cover with the rest of the pastry, pressing down the edges firmly. Brush with beaten egg mixed with a little salt. Make a slit in the middle and put round a few decorative pastry leaves. Leave for a short time for the pastry to "rest". Bake in a pre-heated hot oven for about 40 minutes. Cover the pastry with damp greaseproof paper or foil if it is browning too much.

STEAKS (4)

4 thick fillet or rump steaks
Knob of butter, tbsp olive oil
4 tbsp red wine, 4 tbsp port
4 tbsp double cream
Salt, pepper

Sauté steaks in a sauté or frying pan in the butter and oil, pressing them flat till cooked – about 5 minutes on each side. Add wine and port to the pan and stir to incorporate the pan juices. Boil rapidly until reduced a little. Add cream, bring to the boil and pour over the steaks. Season.

STEAKS WITH HORSERADISH (2)

2 fillet or rump steaks
Nut of butter, dsp olive oil
2 tbsp horseradish cream
2 tbsp crème fraîche or cream
Salt and pepper

Cook the steaks in a nut of butter and little olive oil, pressing them down well, for about 5 minutes on each side. Remove and keep warm. Add 2 tbsp each of horseradish cream and crème fraîche with plenty of seasoning. Pour over the steaks and serve at once – with oven chips and a green salad for a quick and delicious meal.

STILTON SOUP

1 lb (450g) mashed potato
10 oz (275g) stale Stilton cheese
1 pint (570 ml) milk
Coriander or parsley, chopped
Ground black pepper

Crumble the cheese and mix with the mashed potato and milk in a mixer, if possible.   Season with ground black pepper.   Reheat and serve with chopped coriander or, failing that, parsley.

This is a good way of using up stale Stilton cheese after Christmas, but it is not really worth making unless you already have the mashed potato. I keep any left over mashed potato in the freezer and it soon adds up to enough. Otherwise instant mashed potato is quite all right if you add seasoning – pepper rather than salt.

SUMMER PUDDING

2 lb (900g) mixed fruit – raspberries, blackcurrants,
    blackberries, redcurrants etc.
4 oz (110g) granulated sugar
White loaf – not too fresh

Pudding bowl – 1½ pint size

Prepare the fruit and cook with the sugar gently for about 10 minutes.   Leave to cool. Cut about six slices from the bread, removing the crusts and two rounds to fit the bottom and top of the basin. Place a small round in the base of the basin and line the sides with the slices of bread, cutting them to fit so there are no gaps.   Put the fruit in the basin to almost fill the bowl, keeping back any remaining juice to use later. Put the large round on the top to fill the basin.   Put the bowl on a plate with an edge and top the bowl with a saucer or plate that presses down onto the bread. Place a weight on top and leave in the fridge overnight.

The next day, turn out carefully and cover any remaining white pieces of bread with the juice.

Serve with a pouring cream.

TABBOULEH (4)

4 oz (110g) bulgar wheat
4 tbsp lemon juice
4 tomatoes
Red and green pepper
6 spring onions
Dressing: 2 tbsp parsley, 2 tbsp mint
                  2 tbsp olive oil, ½ tsp salt
                  Pinch coriander and cumin

Boil 8 fl oz (225 ml) water, pour over the bulgar wheat, stir in the lemon juice and leave for about 30 minutes, until all the water has been absorbed.   Skin, de-seed and chop the tomatoes and peppers and slice the spring onions. Add the vegetables to the bulgar wheat.   Whisk the olive oil, salt and spices together, add the herbs and pour over the other ingredients.   Stir well, put into an attractive bowl and cover with cling film.   Leave in the fridge until needed.

The advantage of this salad is that it can be made well in advance.

TAGLIATELLE AXIDIE   (8 – 9)

Tagliatelle made with 12oz (335g) flour – see under "Pasta", page 141 or
   1 lb (900g) ready-made tagliatelle
4 oz (110g) mushrooms
8 oz (225g) cold meats – e.g. salami and/or pork and ham

Sauce:
   2 oz (50g) butter or margarine
   2 oz (50g) flour
   1 pint (570 ml) milk, infused with carrot, onion, garlic,
       mace, bay leaf, peppercorns
  Packet of mozzarella (buffalo) cheese
   2 – 3 tbsp cream

Topping: Grated Parmesan cheese

Infuse the milk by bringing slowly to the boil with flavourings added.   Leave with lid on.   Chop the meat into small pieces and slice the mushrooms and cook in a little butter.   Cook the sauce by melting the butter, adding the flour, cooking for one to two minutes and then straining on the milk. Stir and bring to the boil making sure there are no lumps.   Once it has boiled remove from the heat and add the sliced mozzarella.   Season and add a little cream. Cook the tagliatelle, drain and mix in with the sauce immediately. Put in a large fireproof dish or two small ones (one to freeze) and cover with freshly grated Parmesan.

Reheat in a hot oven and serve with a salad.

We had a similar dish to this in an outdoor seaside restaurant at Hotel Axidie in Italy.

TAPENADE

6 – 8 oz (175g – 225g) black olives, pitted
Large clove garlic
3 tbsp capers
8 anchovy fillets, rinsed in milk
4 tbsp olive oil
Pinch cayenne
Few thyme leaves

Peel and crush the garlic and put in a mixer with the olives, capers, drained anchovy fillets, pinch of cayenne and a few chopped herb leaves.   Mix very briefly.   Add the olive oil and give it another quick mix.   Leave in a jar in the fridge.   Spread on biscuits to serve with drinks.

TARAMASALATA

1 – 2 tins smoked cod's roe or 6 oz (175g) fresh, skinned*
3 oz (75g) unsalted butter
Tbsp tomato juice
2 tbsp olive oil
3 tbsp fresh white breadcrumbs
Juice of ½ lemon, clove garlic.
Black pepper

Smoked cod's roe is difficult to buy but you can find it in tins

Put the cod's roe in a mixer with the butter, the breadcrumbs, a crushed clove of garlic and the juice of half a lemon.   Mix and then add the olive oil very slowly until well blended.   Add some black pepper and taste for seasoning.   Serve with toast or biscuits.

TARTARE SAUCE (DEVIL)*

8 heaped tbsp good bottled mayonnaise
Tbsp capers, tbsp gherkins
Tbsp black olives
Clove garlic, shallot
Tbsp parsley, chopped (optional)
Seasoning

Good with fish and also useful as a dip

Drain and rinse the capers, chop the gherkins and olives and mix into the mayonnaise together with the crushed garlic and chopped parsley.   Finally, taste for seasoning, and add salt and pepper if necessary.   Keep in an airtight jar in the fridge.

TARTE BASQUAISE*

Pastry:

6 oz (175g) plain flour, salt
3 oz (75g) butter
2 tbsp water

Filling:

Large red or Spanish onion
2 cloves garlic
Knob butter, tbsp oil
2 oz (50g) fresh breadcrumbs
2 eggs
½ pint (150 ml) milk or milk and cream
2 oz (50g) fresh breadcrumbs
6 tomatoes
2 sweet peppers (red, yellow or orange)
Salt, pepper, nutmeg

Topping:

5 tbsp grated Parmesan cheese

9" (22 cm) flan dish

*** This makes an attractive vegetarian dish**

Make the pastry either in the magimix or by hand. Cut the butter into pieces and mix with the flour and little salt. Add the water to make a firm dough.   Roll out and line a greased 9 inch (22 cm) flan dish and put in the fridge while making the filling. Pre-heat the oven to 190C/375F/Gas 5.

Cook the crushed cloves of garlic and the onions, sliced, in butter and oil until soft for about ten mins. Prepare the breadcrumbs and add to the eggs whisked with the milk. Cut the peppers into slices and simmer in boiling water for 5 mins.   Dip the tomatoes in boiling water and then in cold, to skin them. Cut into quarters, remove the seeds and cut again. Add the onions, peppers and tomatoes, together with plenty of seasoning to the milk mixture and put in the flan case.   Sprinkle over the Parmesan cheese. Put the flan dish on a baking sheet and cook in the hot oven for 40 minutes until set and brown.

Serve with a green salad. This dish can be frozen and reheated after defrosting.

TURKEY – ROAST

12 – 13 lb (5 - 6 kg) Turkey (dressed weight)
Stuffing:
    See under apricot, page 6 and chestnut, page 35

1 lb (450g) chipolata sausages
8 oz (225g) streaky bacon

1 lb (450g) potatoes
1 lb (450g) parsnips

  Bread Sauce – see page 25

Remove any innards from the turkey and make some stock for the gravy by adding water, a slice of carrot and onions and some peppercorns and herbs. Strain and put on one side. Put the turkey in a large roasting tin, stuff the neck with apricot stuffing and the body with chestnut stuffing. Place some streaky bacon over the breast.

Cook the bird in a pre-heated oven 160C/325F/Gas 3 for 4 hours. Par-boil potatoes and parsnips for about 3 minutes and cook in hot fat in a shallow roasting tin for about an hour. Wind pieces of streaky bacon round the sausages and cook round the turkey about ¾ hour before the end of the cooking time. Remove them and the turkey and leave to "rest" in a warm place while making the gravy. Remove some of the fat from the pan, add 2 – 3 tablespoons flour, mix well and leave to brown. Stir in the stock with seasoning and a little wine, Worcester sauce etc. Bring up to the boil and simmer. Strain into a gravy boat.

Ham and Cumberland sauce goes well with turkey.

TZATZIKI

Small carton of natural yoghurt
Cucumber
5 fl oz (150 ml) olive oil
Tbsp white wine vinegar
Chopped dill
Salt and pepper
Sliver of garlic, finely chopped

Slice the cucumber, remove the seeds and cut into small pieces. Add a little salt and leave to drain in a colander. Mix the yoghourt with the olive oil, the garlic, very finely chopped and a tablespoon of white wine vinegar. Season with ground pepper. Pour over the drained and wiped cucumber.

  Serve with curries.

VEAL AND HAM PIE

1½ lb (675g) stewing veal
8 oz (225g) gammon
Tin condensed mushroom soup
Little milk or stock
Salt and pepper
8 oz (225g) puff pastry (frozen or ready-made)

Cut up the gammon into small pieces and add to the pieces of veal. Put in a casserole dish and add a tin of condensed mushroom soup diluted with a little milk or stock and some seasoning. Cover and cook in a moderate oven for about 2 hours.

Place in a pie dish with a pie funnel and cover with the pastry. Make a slit in the centre above the funnel and decorate with pastry leaves. Brush with milk. Cook in a hot oven for about 40 minutes. If the pastry starts to brown, cover with a piece of damp greaseproof paper.

VEAL, EGG AND HAM PIE

1 lb (450g) stewing veal*
8 oz (225g) bacon or bacon pieces
2 eggs, hard-boiled
5 fl oz (150 ml) good stock or consommé
Tbsp sherry or Madeira, 2 tsp gelatine
Chopped parsley, seasoning
Pastry: 12 oz (335g) plain flour
        Tsp salt
        4½ oz (125g) lard
        7 fl oz (200 ml) water
6" (15 cm) loose-bottomed cake tin

You can, of course, use pork instead of the stewing veal

Cut the veal into small pieces and add to the bacon pieces together with the chopped parsley and plenty of seasoning. Hard boil the eggs, shell and leave in cold water. Make up the pastry by putting the lard with the water in a small saucepan. Melt the lard and then bring up to the boil. The moment it is boiling pour onto the flour and salt and beat well with a wooden spoon to form a ball. Working quickly, take two-thirds of the dough and line the cake tin bringing it up the sides. Put half the filling into the tin, add the eggs and then the rest of the filling. Pat the remaining dough into a circle and put on the top pressing the edges firmly together. Make a hole in the centre of the pie. Decorate with a few pastry leaves around the hole in the top. Stand the pie on a baking sheet with an edge and brush over the top with beaten egg. Put the pie in a pre-heated oven at 200C/400F/Gas 6 for 15 minutes, then reduce the heat to 170C/325F/Gas 3 and cook for 2 hours. Remove the pie and leave to cool in the tin. Melt the gelatine in the stock with the sherry and before it sets, pour it into the pie using a pie funnel. Turn out when completely cold.

Leave the pie in the fridge. It will keep well, but will not freeze, due to the eggs, which harden in the freezer. This is fun to make!

VEAL ESCALOPES (4)

4 escalopes of veal
Knob of butter, tbsp olive oil
2 tbsp marsala or sherry

Tomato sauce:
    Tin chopped tomatoes – 400g size
    Knob of butter
    2 cloves garlic
    Onion
    Bay leaf, thyme and/or basil
    Salt and pepper
    5 fl oz (150 ml) strong stock or consommé

First make the sauce by finely chopping the onion and frying in butter for a few minutes. Then add the tomatoes, the crushed cloves of garlic, the herbs and some seasoning.   Simmer for about ten minutes and then add the stock and continue simmering for about 15 minutes. Strain.

Fry the veal in butter and oil for 3 minutes on each side, pressing down well.   Drain and put in a large flat ovenproof dish. Sprinkle with a little marsala or sherry.   Spoon the sauce over the veal and either serve at once or cover with foil and reheat in a hot oven for about 20 minutes.

This can be put together in the morning and cooked in the oven in the evening.

VEAL FRICASSEE (4 – 6)

2 lb (900g) stewing veal*
8 oz (225g) baby onions or shallots
8 oz (225g) baby mushrooms
2 oz (50g) butter, 2 oz (50g) flour
Thyme, parsley stalks, bay leaf
15 fl oz (450 ml) chicken stock
Salt and pepper
Tbsp cream or sour cream
Chopped parsley

Neck is ideal for this recipe, but it is very hard to obtain

Cut the veal in neat pieces. Heat the butter in a flameproof casserole on a low heat and add the peeled onions, the baby mushrooms and the veal.   Coat with the butter and then add the flour. Cook for a minute or two and then add stock (or water and stock cube) to cover.   Bring to the boil and add herbs and seasoning.   Transfer to the oven with a lid and cook at 180C/350F/Gas 4 for about 1½ hours.   Finally add some cream and chopped parsley.

 Serve with new potatoes and a green vegetable.

VEAL WITH CREAM (3)

12 oz (335g) escalope of veal
2 oz (50g) butter, tbsp oil
4 oz (110g) mushrooms
Green pepper, onion
10 fl oz (300 ml) crème fraîche or cream
3 tbsp red wine
Tbsp brandy
Salt and pepper

Cut the veal into strips.   Slice the onion and mushrooms and de-seed the pepper and cut into thin strips. In a frying pan sauté the onions and pepper in a knob of butter and little oil. Then add the mushrooms and cook for a few minutes.   Remove the vegetables, add a little more butter and oil and fry the veal for about 5 minutes.   Return the vegetables, add the red wine, crème fraîche, brandy and seasoning. Stir carefully and bring to the boil.

Serve at once with rice or noodles and a salad.

VEGETABLE CURRY (4)

1 lb (450g) potatoes
8 oz (225g) carrots
2 sticks celery
Onion, apple
8 oz (225g) courgettes
1 oz (25g) fat, tbsp flour
2 tbsp curry powder
2 tbsp tomato ketchup
Tbsp lemon juice
Seasoning

Peel the carrots and cut into sticks.   Put in a large saucepan of water with salt and bring to the boil. Cover and simmer for 5 minutes. Meanwhile peel the potatoes and cut into small cubes. Add to the carrots and simmer covered for about 10 minutes.   Drain and keep 25 fl oz (750 ml) of the liquid. Melt the fat in the saucepan and add sliced celery, onion and apple.   Fry for a few minutes until brown. Add the flour and curry powder and cook for 5 minutes.   Add the vegetable liquid, the tomato ketchup and the lemon juice and bring to the boil.   Cover and simmer for 15 minutes. Add the carrots, potatoes, and courgettes.   Cover and cook for a further 15 minutes, stirring occasionally. Taste for seasoning and serve with rice.

This can be served on its own or with other curries. Different vegetables could be used.

VEGETABLE PIE (8)

4 large onions
1 lb (450g) carrots
12 oz (325g) button mushrooms
Cauliflower
2 oz (50g) butter
Chopped mint, seasoning
Sauce:
    1½ oz (35g) butter
    1½ oz (35g) flour
    15 fl oz (450 ml) flavoured milk
    5 tbsp grated cheese
Topping:
    Mashed potato
    Beaten egg

For this recipe you need a very large flat ovenware dish.   Slice the onions and carrots. Cook the onions in butter. Cook carrots in water with a knob of butter, salt and a teaspoon of sugar until tender. Cook the mushrooms in butter.   Steam the cauliflower in florets.   Put a layer of onions in the ovenware dish, cover with carrots and chopped mint and top with cauliflower and mushrooms. Melt butter, add flour, strain on the flavoured milk (bay leaf, mace, parsley, garlic, peppercorns). Stir, bring to the boil, add the cheese and remove from the heat. Pour over the vegetables. Make some mashed potatoes (instant are fine) and pipe across the top and round the sides.   Brush with beaten egg yolk. Reheat for an hour in a moderate to hot oven.

Can be frozen in which case thaw well before reheating.   Good with baked ham.   Although not difficult to make, this recipe does take a long time and it really does need to be made in advance!

VEGETABLE SOUP

1 oz (25g) dripping, lard or oil
1 lb (450g) vegetables:
   potato, celery stalk, carrot, parsnip, onion etc
2 pts (1.1 litre) stock or water and stock cubes
Seasoning and herbs

Croutons – see page 57

Peel the vegetables and cut into small pieces.   Sweat in the fat in a large saucepan with the lid on for about 10 minutes. without browning.   Add the stock, seasoning and any available herbs. Bring to the boil and simmer for 30 minutes.   Serve as it is or liquidise or sieve.   If it is too thick, add a little cream or milk. Taste for seasoning.   Serve croutons separately – these could have been frozen and can be reheated in the oven.   This soup can, of course, be made with any vegetables, but I think it is better to make it in the winter with root vegetables and make a minestrone soup in the summer.

VENISON AND BEEF CASSEROLE (6)*

1 lb (450g) Venison – preferably haunch
2 lb (900g) chuck steak, cubed
2 raw Chorizo sausages, sliced
2 tbsp dripping or fat
2 tbsp flour, 1 tbsp tomato puree
Stick of celery, bay leaf
2 onions, sliced
2 cloves garlic, crushed
Tin of plum tomatoes – 400g size
Beef stock cube and seasoning
8 oz (225g) mushrooms
½ pint (10 fl oz) red wine

This recipe needs to be started two days ahead

Cut the venison into cubes and marinade overnight in the red wine, chopped celery and bay leaf.

The next day drain the venison, keeping back the marinade. Put the fat in a large casserole dish, which also goes on the stove and fry the sliced onions, crushed garlic and cubed venison and steak until well browned.   Add two tbsp heaped flour and a tbsp tomato puree. Cook for a minute or two, then add the tin of plum tomatoes with their juice, the wine from the marinade, the mushrooms (sliced if large) and a crumbled beef stock cube, together with the sliced chorizo sausages. Stir and bring to the boil. Transfer to a moderate oven (170C/350F/Gas 4) for about 2 hours.   Remove and leave overnight.

The following day reheat in a moderate to hot oven for up to an hour. Serve with baked potatoes and a green vegetable.

VIENNESE BISCUITS

6 oz (175g) unsalted butter
5 oz (150g) plain flour
1 oz (25g) cornflour
2 oz (25g) icing sugar
Tsp vanilla extract
Glacé cherries
Flaked almonds

Cream the butter and sugar together.   Add the flours and mix adding a drop of milk if necessary. Grease some large baking sheets and put the mixture into a piping bag with large star tube. Pipe out rounds or fingers or, if you do not like using a piping bag, put out in teaspoonfuls. Cover the centre of the rounds with pieces of glacé cherries and/or flaked almonds.   Leave in fridge to chill for about 10 minutes before baking. Bake in moderate oven (180C/350F/Gas 4) for 10 – 15 mins. Watch carefully and remove when starting to brown. Cool in the tin before removing to a wire rack. Keep in an airtight tin or freeze. The fingers can be dipped in melted chocolate.

VOL-AU-VENT

Vol-au-Vent cases – small size for cocktails
                    large size for luncheon

Fillings:
    Ham and/or chicken and mushrooms – see pancakes, page 138
    Lobster – see lobster vol-au-vent, page 110
    Prawn – see pancakes, page 139
    Scallops – see following recipe

If using frozen vol-au-vent cases, which I recommend, cook according to the instructions on the packet.   Leave to cool, take off the lids and remove any soggy pastry from the centre.

Make the sauce and leave to get cold.   Put the cases on a baking sheet and fill with the cold filling, pressing down well.   Put on the lids.

When needed reheat in a hot oven.   Serve the tiny ones with drinks and the large ones with vegetables and/or a salad as a main course.

VOL-AU-VENT WITH SCALLOPS

Per person:

2 large vol-au-vent cases, cooked
2 scallops
2 oz (50g) mushrooms
2 tomatoes, skinned and diced
1 oz (25g) butter
Tsp tomato puree
Tbsp sherry
Egg yolk
5 fl oz (150 ml) cream (or crème fraîche)
Salt, pepper, lemon juice, parsley

Clean the scallops and cut in half. Cook in a little butter with seasoning on a low heat for ten mins. Slice the mushrooms and cook in a knob of butter in another pan for a few minutes. Add the sherry, tomatoes and the mushrooms to the scallops.   Mix the cream with the egg yolk and add to the mixture.   Do not boil. Add some chopped parsley and lemon juice. Taste for seasoning.

About half an hour before ready to eat reheat the cases in a hot oven.   Reheat the scallops on top of the stove for a short time – stirring well and removing before they boil – and pour into and over the hot cases.   Serve with vegetables to make an interesting main course.

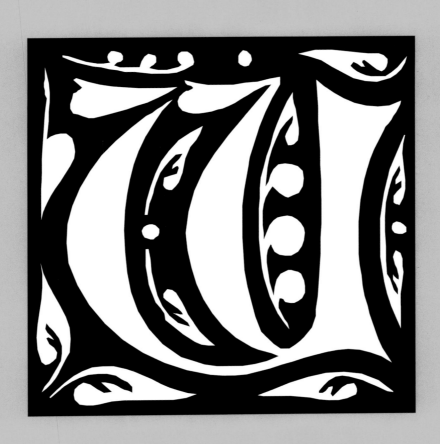

WALDORF SALAD

1 celery
2 crisp apples
Handful of broken walnuts

French dressing – see page 73

Cut celery into small pieces and slice the apples, leaving on their skins. Mix together with the walnuts. Mix with about 3 tablespoons of French dressing. Leave in the fridge until needed.

This salad is quick to make and does not have to be eaten at once.

WATERCRESS CREAM SALAD

2 bunches or packets Watercress
3 tbsp cream
Juice of 1 lemon
Salt and pepper

Topping:
    2 oz (50g) pine nuts

Wash and drain the watercress, removing hard stalks. Or buy 2 packets of ready prepared watercress from a supermarket, in which case, it is not necessary to wash it. Mix the lemon juice, the cream and seasoning. Mix with the watercress, top with the pine nuts and serve.

WELSH RAREBIT (2)

2 large slices of bread
1 oz (25g) butter
1 tbsp flour
4 tbsp milk or 2 tbsp milk and 2 tbsp ale
4 oz (110g) mature Cheddar cheese
Tsp Worcester sauce
Tsp mustard powder
Ground pepper

Grate the cheddar cheese. Toast the slices of bread and put on a low sided tin ready to go under the grill. Melt the butter, add the flour, cook a little and pour on the 4 tbsp milk and/or ale. Stir well and add the grated cheese, the Worcester sauce, the mustard and the ground pepper. Mix well until the cheese is almost melted and then pour over the toasts. Put under a hot grill until melted and eat at once.

WHITE SAUCE

1½ oz (35g) butter or margarine
2 tbsp flour
10 fl oz (300 ml) milk
Seasoning

For people like my husband who are not used to making white sauce this is an infallible recipe. Put 1½ oz (35g) butter in a small saucepan and melt over a low heat.   Stir in two tablespoons of flour and stir well for about a minute. Add the milk, stir and heat the milk, but do not boil.   Turn off the heat and leave it to amalgamate. When needed stir the sauce, making sure there are no lumps and bring it to the boil, stirring all the time.   Remove from the heat and add salt and pepper. If there should be some lumps because it has boiled before they have all been removed, you can always sieve it!

By adding a handful of chopped parsley you have a Parsley Sauce and by adding some grated cheese, with a little mustard, you have a Sauce Mornay

WILD DUCK

2 wild duck*
Onion, carrot and 2 stalks celery
Sauce:
   2 oz (50g) butter
   Onion, sliced
   Clove garlic, crushed
   2 heaped tbsp flour and tbsp tomato puree
   4 oz (110g) sliced mushrooms
   Orange juice and rind
   Tbsp red currant jelly
   4 tbsp red wine
   4 tbsp crème fraîche
   Seasoning

In season September 1st – January 31st

Cook two ducks in a roasting tin surrounded by water with a chopped onion, pieces of carrot and slices of celery and some herbs and a bay leaf.   Cover with foil and cook in a moderate oven for 1½ hrs.   Remove from the oven, strain off the stock and use 8 fl oz (225 ml) for the sauce.

Make the sauce by cooking a sliced onion and crushed glove of garlic in the fat and stirring in the flour and tomato puree. Cook for a minute and then add the sliced mushrooms, the stock, the juice and the rind of the orange, the redcurrant jelly and the wine. Bring to the boil and finally add the crème fraîche.

Bone the ducks and place in an ovenproof serving dish.   Pour over the sauce, cover with foil and reheat in a moderate oven at least for 40 minutes.

YOGHOURT WITH APRICOTS (2)

½ pint (300 ml) Greek yoghourt
4 oz (110g) dried apricots
2 tsp liquid honey

Chop the apricots and mix into the yoghourt and leave to stand overnight, if possible, to soften. Stir in the honey and mix and put into two glasses or bowls. Leave in fridge until needed.

YORKSHIRE PUDDING

5 oz (150g) plain flour
Salt
2 small eggs
10 fl oz (300 ml) milk or milk and water

Mix eggs and half of the liquid with the flour, stirring gradually and then beating well. Finally, add the rest of the liquid, cover with cling film and leave to rest for at least half an hour.

Put some hot fat from the joint in either a large tin or individual tins and put on the top shelf of a hot oven. Do not use a fan oven when cooking a Yorkshire pudding. Leave for a few minutes before pouring in the batter.

Leave until well risen and brown and ready to come out of the tin – if it is sticking it is not ready. It should take about 15 minutes for individual ones and 45 minutes for a whole pudding.